Contents

v

Introduction

A Closer Look provides students with an opportunity to review and practice grammatical items which are normally included in any basic English course. This book should appeal to:

- students who are currently enrolled in a course and feel the need for additional practice and/or review.
- students who have already completed a basic course and would like to have a summary of what is expected of intermediate level students.
- students who are in advanced courses and need to cover any possible gaps in their English.

Although *A Closer Look* contains a great number and variety of exercises, it would be a mistake, perhaps, to work through the book from cover to cover, front to back. Instead, students should try to identify weaknesses in their own knowledge and work with the book to remedy these problems. They can try to correct these weaknesses by looking up specific points in *A Closer Look*. They can consult the presentation of any grammatical item in question, and then attempt to solve the tasks which follow before they complete the "Check" exercises.

The presentations of the various topics are written in two different ways. In some cases, a simple presentation of the grammar in tables is the clearest, most direct approach. Quite simply, "this is how it is." In some cases, it is necessary to explain what happens with the language. Students need a certain understanding of *why* the language changes and how it works in order to be able to master the particular point.

Because the book is directed at a world-wide audience, many students will find items that seem self-evident and pose no problems at all. Other students will realize that English differs from their own language in some respects and will be pleased to find the differences presented in *A Closer Look*.

Many students will want to work on their own with the book. For this reason, the number of exercises which would function best as pairwork or groupwork is limited. Instead, the focus is on exercises which work well for the *individual* student.

Individualization—giving individual students the chance to practice according to their own needs—is often neglected in class because of a simple lack of material. *A Closer Look* will provide the teacher and student with a wealth of exercises that should cover the individual student's needs ranging from the simple to the complex.

Because it is impossible to know the background and needs of each student using the text, *A Closer Look* offers optional translating. Students may, if they find it helpful, translate words in lists when they come across them for the first time. It may also be useful for students to translate the answers given in the exercises in order to gain a fuller understanding and insight into the differences and similarities between English and their native languages.

A Closer Look should be a valuable source of material for students at various levels of competency.* It should be used as a tool to discover or rediscover and practice many of the various grammatical rules and exceptions in the English language.

*Students using *Intermediate English 1 and 2* will find *A Closer Look* to be an excellent companion book for further clarification of grammar presented in this course.

Part I/Indefinite Articles

1. Presentation **Choosing an indefinite article**

An is used before vowel sounds. *A* is used before all other sounds.

Tom is *an* actor. He is *a* good one too! He has *an* award and *a* diploma from *an* excellent acting school in New York. Tom has acted in *a* play on Broadway and has also acted in *a* film. He used to act in school plays in *an* auditorium in *a* small town where he lived.

Pronunciation, not spelling, determines the use of *a* or *an*.

Tom is *an* honest and hardworking person. He often has to take other jobs when he cannot find acting jobs. He belongs to *a* union so that he can drive cabs and buses. He has to wear *a* uniform to work. Sometimes Tom studies scripts for *an* hour at lunch.

Practice

A. What's Tom's cab like?   yellow   *It's a yellow one.*

1. What's his script like?   boring   It's a boring one

2. What's his hometown like?   small   It's a small one.

3. What's Tom's house like?   white   It's a white one

4. What's his play like?   famous   It's a famous one

B. What's Tom's job like?   interesting   *It's an interesting one.*

1. What's his film like?   exciting   It's an exciting one

2. What's his school like?   excellent   It's an excellent one

3. What's Tom's new uniform like?   orange   It's an orange one

4. What's his award like?   important   It's an important one

1

Check

A. Fill in *a* or *an*.

1. Tom is wearing __*a*__ new uniform.

2. It is __*an*__ orange one.

3. Tom wants to be __*a*__ popular actor.

4. He is __*an*__ honest man.

5. He studies for __*an*__ hour.

6. He often brings __*an*__ interesting script to work.

B. Answer the questions using *a* or *an*.

1. Does the man drive an American car or a European car?

   He drives an European car

2. Where does he drive?

   He drive to a hotel

3. Where does he park?

   he parks at a front of a hotel

4. What is the doorman wearing?

   He's wearing an uniform

5. How long does his car stand there?

   His car stands ther an hour

6. Why doesn't the police officer tow away the car?

   _____

2. Presentation   Using a/an before specific nouns

A and *an* are used before professions, nationalities, religions and political parties.

Rita is *an* artist and her husband, Carl, is *a* reporter. She is *a* Brazilian and he is *an* American. Rita is *a* Catholic, but Carl is *a* Protestant. Carl is *a* Republican but Rita keeps quiet. Carl thinks Rita is *a* Republican too!

Practice

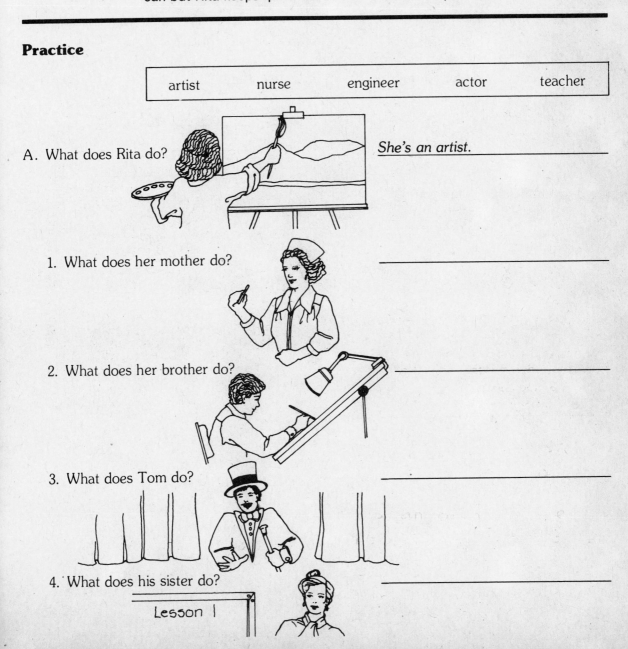

| artist | nurse | engineer | actor | teacher |

A. What does Rita do?   *She's an artist.* _____

1. What does her mother do?   _____

2. What does her brother do?   _____

3. What does Tom do?   _____

4. What does his sister do? _____

Lesson 1

B. Is Rita from Brazil?   Brazilian   *Yes. She's a Brazilian.* _____

   1. Is her mother from Mexico?   Mexican   _____

   2. Is her father from Argentina?   Argentinian _____

   3. Is Carl from America?   American   _____

   4. Is his father from Canada?   Canadian   _____

   5. Is his mother from Italy?   Italian   _____

C. What about *you*?

   1. What do you do for a living?   *I am* _____

   2. What do other members of your
      family do?
                                                              _____

                                                              _____

                                                              _____

   3. What nationality are you?   _____

3. Presentation   Using *a/an* to indicate quantity

Some expressions show "a part of" and are preceded by an indefinite article.

a piece of

a box of

a slice of

a pair of

a ton of

a bar of

a kilo of

a pound of

A/an also show quantity relationships.

Rita works forty weeks *a* year. Carl works eight hours *a* day.
Milk costs a dollar *a* bottle and cheese costs twenty cents *an* ounce.

Practice

A. What's this?

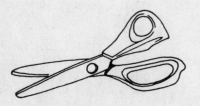

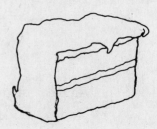

1. *a pair of scissors*   2. _____

3. _____   4. _____

5. _____   6. _____

B. Rita and Carl both work. How long?

   1. Rita works from eight until six. How many hours a day?
   She works for ten hours a day.

   2. Carl works from twelve until eight. How many hours a day?

   _____

   3. They work from Monday to Saturday. How many days a week?

   _____

   4. They don't work from June to September. How many months a year?

   _____

C. Rita and Carl shop each week. How much?

1. *It costs seventy-five cents a bottle.*

2. _____

3. _____

4. _____

D. Rita and Carl pay their bills. How much?

1. How much does the rent cost?
   ($400/month) *It costs four hundred dollars a month.*

2. How much does the newspaper cost?
   ($2.00/week) _____

3. How much does the telephone cost?
   ($20/month) _____

4. How much does their tennis club membership cost?
   ($430/year) _____

4. Presentation   Special phrases using *a/an*

Use the verb *to have* plus *a/an* and complaint.

Ann has *a* cough and *an* earache. Her son, Jason, has *an* infection and *a* temperature.

Some common phrases use *a/an*.

Ann goes to the museum once a week on *an average*. *As a rule*, she never misses the modern art exhibits. *It's a pity* she can't go today.

Jason looks quite healthy *at a distance*. *It's a shame* that he is not feeling well today. But, he still has *a big appetite*. He's *in a hurry* to get well!

Practice

Complete the following sentences.

a cold	a fever	a broken leg
a big appetite	an earache	an infection

1. Ann has ____*a cold*____.

2. Jason has _____.

3. He also has _____ in his throat.

4. Last month Ann had _____ .

5. She has _____ .

6. My dog has _____ .

Check

Answer these questions with some of the common phrases you have just learned.

Did you hear that Ann had lost her dog?   _Yes, what a pity._____

1. Why is Ann running?   _____

2. Do you always get up at seven o'clock?   _____

3. Why did Ann call a doctor?   _____

4. Why does Jason eat so much?   _____

5. Presentation   *A/an* with count nouns

A or *an* are placed after *half*, *such* and *quite* when they stand before count nouns.

Peter is *such an* idiot! Why did he ever buy *such an* old car? It only has *half an* engine. It is *quite a* sight to see!

A/an are used after exclamations with *what* before count nouns.

When Peter bought the car, he exclaimed, "*What a* nice car! *What an* unusual engine! *What a* great deal!"

A/an are <u>not</u> used before nouns which cannot be counted or are plural.

Peter's friends couldn't help saying "*Such* dirty upholstery! *What* filthy paint!" But Peter smiled and continued to look at the engine and said, "*Such* interesting wires! *What* wonderful cables . . ."

Practice

A. Don't you think it's a wonderful car?   *It's quite a wonderful car!*_____

   1.   a low price?   _____

   2. Don't you think it's an unusual engine?   _____

   3.   a good buy?   _____

   4.   an interesting car?   _____

B. Would you like a can of oil?   *Just half a can.*_____

   1.   a bucket of water?   _____

   2. Would you like a box of screws?   _____

   3.   a can of paint?   _____

   4.   a glass of beer?   _____

C. Do you think Peter is a good mechanic?   *Oh, he's such a good mechanic!*____

   1.   it's a great bargain?   _____

   2. Do you think Peter is a good friend?   _____

   3.   Peter is a smart person?   _____

   4.   it's an unbelievable car?   _____

Check

A	AN	—
		✓

A. What • beautiful flowers!

1. He is such • interesting person!

2. Just half • cup, please.

3. They are quite • nice people.

4. The children are such • good students.

5. "What • fine wheels!" he exclaimed.

6. I've never heard such • nonsense.

7. What • terrible weather!

8. What • awful storm!

B. Is this a pretty hat?

1. Is this a good idea?

2. Is that an interesting book?

3. Are they nice people?

4. Are the shoes cheap?

5. Is this coffee strong?

What a pretty hat! _____

_____

_____

_____

_____

_____

C. What are they saying?

Part II/Definite Article

1. Presentation **Pronunciation of** *the*

The is used before both singular and plural words.

Singular: the boy, the girl
Plural: the boys, the girls

The *e* in *the* is pronounced [e]—the *e* as in *easy*—before vowel sounds.

Detective Miller interviewed *the* owner of *the* antique store. He questioned him about *the* absence of several hundred expensive vases. Apparently, *the* unbelievable robbery took place just after midnight.

The *e* in *the* is pronounced [ə]—the *a* as in *about*—before all other sounds.

The thief broke into the store. He stole *the* vases which were displayed in *the* cabinets along *the* wall. He plans to sell all of *the* valuable vases to many different antique dealers across *the* country.

The is pronounced [e] to indicate something is special or unique.

This crime is *the* biggest event of 1983. That antique store is *the* most respected one in the country!

Practice

A. Read these sentences.

1. The owner lost all the antique vases.

2. They were in the old cabinets.

3. The investigator discovered only one fingerprint.

4. The unusual robbery occurred last night.

5. The owner of the antique store is quite upset.

12

B. Now read these sentences.

1. The thief stole over four hundred vases.

2. The vases were made by native American Indians.

3. The quality of these vases was quite magnificent.

4. The detective is trying to solve the mystery.

5. The fingerprint is his only clue!

Check

Choose the correct sound.

(easy) e	(about) ə

1. *The* detective has been investigating this robbery for over a week.

2. *The* vases still cannot be found.

3. *The* owner has offered a reward.

4. *The* police think there is a witness to this crime.

5. *The* only thing to do is to wait.

6. Perhaps a witness will want to claim *the* reward.

7. *The* detective is baffled by this mystery.

8. How could one thief carry 479 vases out of *the* store?

2. Presentation   Normal usage of *the*

The usually precedes a word followed by *of*.

The title *of* the book is Henry: *The* King *of* England. *The* size *of* the book is quite large, and *the* end *of* the story is well worth waiting for!

The precedes adjectives in the superlative.

The Empire State building is one of *the* tallest buildings in New York. But, the World Trade buildings are *the* tallest.

The precedes proper names in the plural.

The Sheehans live in Reading and the Dandisons own a house in Lexington.

The is used before names of rivers, ships, theaters, oceans, hotels and newspapers.

The Fords traveled to England on *the* Queen Elizabeth II. They sailed across *the* Atlantic and arrived in London for a month's vacation. The Fords stayed at *the* Savoy and enjoyed their time there. Every morning they would have breakfast in bed and read *the* London Times. They sailed on *the* Thames and attended shows at *the* Paladium too.

The is used before adjectives used as nouns.

Robin Hood always stole from *the* rich and gave to *the* poor.

The is used before the names of musical instruments and radio, movies and telephone.

Paul McCartney plays the guitar and his wife, Linda, plays the piano. I often hear their songs on *the* radio and have even gone to *the* movies to see a film about their last concert tour.

Practice

A. What about you? Who or what is the most . . . ?

1. Who is the most interesting student in class?

_____ *is the most interesting student in class.*

2. What is the most popular restaurant in town?

_____

3. What is the most difficult subject in school?

_____

4. What is the most boring sport?

_____

5. What is the most fascinating subject in school?

_____

6. Who is the most beautiful/handsome student in school?

_____

B. What do the McCartneys read?   *London Free Press*

The McCartneys read the London Free Press.

1. Where is Paris?   Seine

_____

2. What do the Brynes read?   *New York Times*

_____

3. Where is Rome?   Tiber

_____

4. What instrument does Burt play?   piano

_____

5. What instrument does Ringo play?   drums

_____

6. What do the Donahues read?   *Chicago Sun*

_____

Check

A. Find the correct answers to these questions using the following vocabulary.

President	Ritz	flute	Queen
Hudson	*Tribune*	deaf	Shubert

1. Who did you see in London? _I saw the Queen._

2. Where is New York? _____

3. What instrument does she play? _____

4. Who did you see at the White House? _____

5. Who is she always helping? _____

6. What theater did you go to? _____

7. Where did you stay in Boston? _____

8. What newspaper do they read? _____

B. Now find the correct answers to these questions.

Titanic	piano	Builtmore
Times	Charles	Warwick

1. Where is Boston? _____

2. What instrument does John play? _____

3. What ship did they travel on? _____

4. Where is the movie playing? _____

5. Where did you stay in Los Angeles? _____

6. What newspaper does he read? _____

3. Presentation   Placement of the definite article

The is used <u>before</u> certain words.

Rosa was going away to school for *the first* time. *The usual* way to get to her school was by train. Rosa arrived at the train station at *the beginning* of rush hour. She walked in one direction and then in *the opposite* direction. She asked a stranger about *the right* way to the ticket window. Rosa soon discovered that she was on *the wrong* train! She ran out of that train and found *the correct* one. Rosa promised herself that this would be *the last* time she took a train to school. *The next* time she will probably take the bus to school!

The is used <u>after</u> certain words.

Rosa had to pay *twice the* amount for the train ticket than she had planned. She used *all the* money that she had in her purse. She also had to take *both the* aspirins she brought with her because she had such a headache!

Practice

A. Complete these sentences using some of the phrases shown above.

Rosa took the bus _____*the first*_____ time she went to school. The bus went _____ way until it reached Albany. The bus driver took _____ turn. He had to go back in _____ direction. Rosa got to school very late. Now, she promised herself that this would be _____ time she took the bus. She'd drive her own car from now on!

B. Is there any money left?   *All the money is gone.* _____

1.   time   _____

2. Are there any aspirins left?   _____

3.   tickets   _____

C. There are two checks for Rosa.   *She took both the checks.*

    1.   tickets   _____

    2. There are two aspirins for Rosa.   _____

    3.   sandwiches   _____

Check

A. Fill in *the* where necessary.

Rosa was angry because she had to pay _____ twice _____ price for her train ticket and had a difficult time finding _____ right _____ way to the ticket window. She had spent _____ all _____ money she had with her. Rosa thought that she should take the bus _____ next _____ time. That wasn't much better! The bus was very late because the driver went in _____ opposite _____ direction. That would be _____ last _____ time she took the bus!

B. What are they saying? Match the speakers with their "bubbles."

4. Presentation   No definite article

The is usually <u>not used</u> before the following:

Days/time designations:

I saw your friend, Jean, *on* Monday. She said that she will call you *next* week. She bought a new car *last* month and wants you to see it.

Holidays/festivals:

Bill doesn't have to work *at* Easter and *on* Christmas Day. He plans to take a vacation and go to Mardi Gras in New Orleans this year.

Meals:

Elaine would like fish and french fries *for* dinner. She would like some ice cream *for* dessert.

No definite article is used with the names of meals unless a special meal or the food is referred to:

The President was present at *the* dinner. He thought that *the* roast beef was delicious and complimented the chef for *the* wonderful meal.

Or with streets, parks, certain buildings if the first word is a proper name:

The Giannettos had a picnic lunch in Central Park. Then, they walked down Fifth Avenue to do some shopping. Later that day, they went to the circus at Madison Square Garden.

Note: There are exceptions to this rule, such as: the Strand, the Haymarket, the Embankment, the Mall, the Bronx.

Titles take no definite article when immediately followed by a proper name:

Prince Ferdinand attended a meeting with Queen Isabella, President Baxter and Prime Minister McKenzie.

Note: The is used before the names of professions or trades, such as:

The author, Charles Dickens. Mr. Brady, the butcher. The poet, Anne Sexton.

Practice

Sunday	Monday	Tuesday	Wednesday	Thursday	Friday	Saturday
PARTY AT CAROL'S	TOM		MOTHER		DINNER WITH JEAN	CONCERT WITH LIZ

A. When are you going to see Tom? — _On Monday._

   1. When are you going to the party at Carol's? _____

   2. When are you going to visit your mother? _____

   3. When are you having dinner with Jean? _____

   4. When are you going to the concert with Liz? _____

B. What would Emily like for breakfast?   bacon/eggs   _Emily would like bacon and eggs._

   1.   lunch?   salad   _____

   2.   supper?   sandwiches   _____

   3. What would Emily like for dinner?   fish   _____

   4.   dessert?   pie   _____

C. What did the Giannettos see in New York?

   —What did they see first?

   —Central Park.

   —And then?

   —Greenwich Village.

   —And then?

   —Rockefeller Center.

   —And then?

   —Madison Square Garden.

Now write about *your* favorite place.

   —What did you see first?

   _____

   —And then?

   _____

   —And then?

   _____

   —And then?

   _____

D. Fill in *the* where necessary.

Bill works in a fancy restaurant in San Francisco. He is ___*the*___ waiter in the main dining room. He works hard and has impressed _____ manager of the restaurant. Even _____ owner likes Bill. They give him more and more responsibility each week. Celebrities often come to eat at the restaurant and they always ask for Bill to serve them. One night the restaurant was particularly busy. Bill waited on _____ Queen, _____ governor of California, _____ actor Paul Newman, Carly Simon _____ singer and _____ Sir Lawrence Olivier! Bill will never forget that night!

5. Presentation   Further examples of no definite article

Prepositions and nouns without article

Donna is a lawyer. Sometimes she is so tired when she gets home that she goes immediately *to bed*. She gets up *at dawn*. She likes to hear the birds sing *at sunrise*. Her husband, Gerald, is a doctor. He works *at night*. He likes to sleep *by day*. He usually gets up for lunch *at noon*, and then he likes to lie *in bed* for the rest of the afternoon. He dreams about going *to sea*.

Other prepositional phrases with court, prison, bed, table:

at court, in court, to be sent (to go) to prison, to escape from prison, to be (ill) in bed and to jump out of bed, (to wait) on table.

The is not used when discussing the general purpose of a building.

Donna goes *to school* every morning. Then she has to defend clients *in court* every afternoon. Gerald takes sailing lessons *at school* every summer.

The is used when talking about a specific building.

Donna takes classes at *the school* on Broad Street. It is across the street from *the church* with the white steeple.

Practice

A. Does Donna often go to school?   twice a week   *Donna goes to school twice a week.*

1. Does she usually go to court?   once a day   _____

2. When does Donna usually go to bed?   at 9:00   _____

3. Will Gerald ever go to sea?   in a year   _____

4. Does he ever go to school?   in the summer   _____

B. Where should they meet?

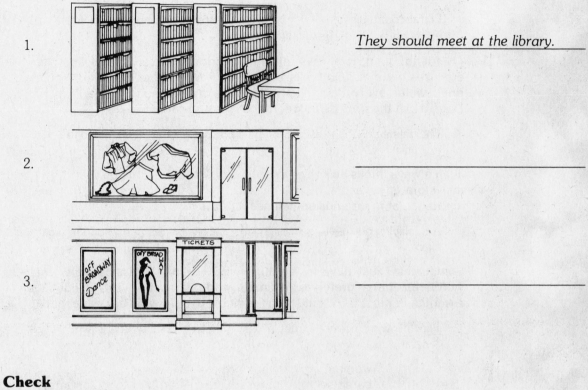

1.   *They should meet at the library.*

2.   _____

3.   _____

Check

Fill in *the* where necessary.

Donna got out of _____ bed at _____ sunrise. The birds were singing and _____ sunrise was very beautiful. Donna loves _____ morning. She likes to eat _____ breakfast and think about her day's work in _____ court. She knows that she has a difficult case ahead of her today. One of her clients may be sent to _____ prison. Donna is very worried about this case.

Gerald came home from work at _____ hospital just as Donna was leaving for _____ courthouse. He is concerned about Donna. He wants to go away on a vacation. He would like to take Donna to _____ sea. Gerald wants to buy a boat and see _____ world! They could travel by _____ day and anchor the boat at _____ sunset each night. _____ spring is the ideal time to travel!

6. Presentation   Choosing when to use the definite article

Plural countables and uncountables if used in an unrestricted sense (=all that exist) do not take the definite article.

My friend, Juan, is always talking. He criticizes everything I do or say. He criticizes my diet: "Coffee is bad for you! Milk is good for you. You should drink water every day." Juan also tells me: "Freedom is a human right! Dogs make the best pets. Ignorance is not always bliss."

The definite article is used if the meaning of the noun is restricted to a particular example.

Juan always thinks he knows the answers. He tells me things like: "The fruit at that store is never fresh. The music on your stereo is simply horrible. The ignorance of my friends sometimes amazes me!"

A qualifying adjective or phrase does not always restrict a noun to a particular example.

Sometimes I just **have** to tell Juan what I think: "Classical music may be wonderful, but I prefer to listen to modern music. College education is essential in most jobs, but I don't criticize people with less education!

The following nouns do not usually take the definite article when used in a general sense:

man	woman	mankind	heaven	hell
fate	paradise	nature	eternity	purgatory
posterity	providence	humanity	antiquity	

Practice

Fill in *the* where necessary.

A. Juan: I love _____ modern art!

Karen: _____ art of the Impressionist period is my favorite.

Juan: I'm glad that you can appreciate _____ art of someone like Van Gogh, because I don't!

Karen: Well, you certainly have _____ freedom to express your opinion.

Juan: I hate it when people say _____ ignorance is bliss.

Karen: I know . . . and how about when people say that _____ blood is thicker than water?

Juan: For your _____ information, you say that to me all the time!

Karen: Well, as you were saying . . . _____ ignorance of your friends is truly amazing!

B. I'd like to buy a pet!   mice   _Mice make good pets!_ _____

   1.   cats   _____

   2.   birds   _____

   3.   horses   _____

   4.   dogs   _____

C. Fill in _the_ where necessary.
   1. _____ love is blind.

   2. For _____ life of me, I can't explain why I like Juan so much.

   3. He does have _____ freedom to state his opinions.

   4. He loves _____ French food at Ferdinands.

   5. I like _____ Italian food.

   6. He loves _____ classical music.

   7. I enjoy _____ jazz of musicians like Dave Brubeck and Chuck Mangione.

   8. _____ good books mean a lot to me.

D. Fill in *the* where necessary.

1. There are many various beliefs held by _____ mankind.

2. In most countries, _____ man and _____ woman are considered equal.

3. On the other hand, many nations believe that _____ man is superior to _____ woman.

4. The concept of _____ heaven and _____ hell is believed by many religions.

5. _____ Christianity had a huge influence on European history.

6. Most Catholics believe in the idea of _____ purgatory.

7. _____ nature of society is a complex issue.

8. _____ fate intends for various things to happen in this world.

9. Some people find _____ paradise they long for.

10. _____ man is his own worst enemy.

E. Fill in *the* where necessary.

1. Wonder washes _____ clothes like no other detergent.

2. It brightens _____ colors.

3. It removes all of _____ stains from all of your clothes.

4. _____ experts have proven how effective this product is by doing many experiments.

5. _____ experiments are scientifically proven.

6. Wonder is _____ best detergent around.

Part III/Nouns

1. Presentation

Classification of nouns

One of the most important ways of classifying nouns is:

Countables—nouns that can be counted like books, trees, dogs

Uncountables—nouns that cannot be counted like meat, gold, grass, wool, goodness, love, hatred, etc. These are things that are primarily names of materials, qualities and sciences.

Within both groups there are *concrete nouns* or words for things we can touch or see and *abstract nouns* or words for qualities or ideas that we cannot touch or see.

Certain nouns can be countables in one sense and uncountables in another.

Countables	Uncountables
He drank out of a glass.	The window is made of glass.
The liquid in the glass is poisonous.	Liquid is necessary for life.

2. Presentation Plural nouns

The plural is usually formed by the addition of -s or -es.

The boy—the boys, class—classes, church—churches

General rules for pronunciation:

-s is pronounced [s] voiceless after voiceless sounds like after f, k, p, t, e and in words like months

-s is pronounced [z] voiced after voiced sounds in words like cars and dogs

A final -es is pronounced [iz] after the following sounds:

glasses [siz]	vases [ziz]	batches [tiez]	horses
pages [dg]	bushes [siz]	languages	sizes

Practice

A. Read these sentences. Listen for the [s] sound.

1. Claire loves cats!

2. Her new cat is only six months old and is always in trouble.

3. Last night the cat climbed up Claire's new drapes.

4. Her cat also breaks all the cups in the kitchen.

5. This cat also smacks his lips when he's hungry!

B. Now read these sentences. Listen for the [z] sound.

1. Claire took some youths on a camping trip last weekend.

2. They hiked on many paths in the forest.

3. The little boys got very dirty and didn't have to take baths.

4. They are all great friends and had a wonderful time.

5. The boys wished that their trip lasted more than two days.

C. Read these sentences. Listen for the [iz] sound.

 1. Claire works hard for her wages.

 2. She edits manuscripts with many pages.

 3. All the books are various sizes.

 4. Claire knows several different languages.

 5. She also attends classes at night.

Check

Choose the correct sound.

	[s]	[z]	[iz]
1. Claire drank two *cups* of coffee for breakfast.			
2. The boys had *eggs* and hot chocolate.			
3. They didn't want to get hungry on the *paths*.			
4. They could have hiked in the *woods* forever.			
5. The boys all wanted to ride *horses* after lunch.			
6. Claire wanted to rest and read a *few pages* of a good book.			
7. But she lost her *glasses* on this trip.			
8. She thinks she dropped them in the *bushes*.			
9. I hate *cats*!			
10. I don't like *dogs* much, either.			
11. I don't get along with animals.			
12. *Pets* are too much trouble.			
13. I have a lot of *plants* instead.			

3. Presentation   Spelling of plural nouns

Words ending in -y:

vowel + y (+s)	consonant + y (y = ies)
day - days	baby - babies
monkey - monkeys	story - stories
key - keys	lady - ladies
boy - boys	library - libraries

Jack often visits the zoo on hot summer *days*. He likes to watch the *monkeys* and *donkeys*. Jack visits the college and public *libraries* on rainy *days*. He likes to read *stories* about various zoo animals.

Words ending in -o:

add -es

hero - heroes	echo - echoes
mosquito - mosquitoes	veto - vetoes
potato - potatoes	torpedo - torpedoes
tomato - tomatoes	embargo - embargoes

However, there are many exceptions to the rule:

photo - photos	tango - tangos
piano - pianos	solo - solos
radio - radios	soprano - sopranos
studio - studios	dynamo - dynamos

Jack prepares dinner for himself quite often. He likes baked *potatoes* with all of his meals. He also enjoys fresh *tomatoes* in his salads. Jack likes to collect *photos* in his pastime; he also repairs old *radios* for his friends.

Some common words ending in -f or -fe:

Replace the -f or -fe with -ves.

calf - calves	thief - thieves
half - halves	wolf - wolves
leaf - leaves	knife - knives
loaf - loaves	life - lives
shelf - shelves	wife - wives

There are exceptions to the rule:

roof - roofs   cliff - cliffs
handkerchief - handkerchiefs   safe - safes

Jack cleans his apartment on Saturdays. He dusts his *bookshelves* and washes his dishes, spoons, forks and *knives*. When Jack finishes his cleaning, he likes to bake several *loaves* of bread for his sandwiches for the week.

Practice

A. Jack is at a big party in New York. Is he having fun?

1.   city.   *He likes cities.* _____

2.   lady.   _____

3. Jack likes the story.   _____

4.   baby.   _____

5.   party.   _____

B. Jack lives in an apartment. How many things are in it?

1.   piano?   *There are several pianos.* _____

2.   photo?   _____

3. Is there only one radio?   _____

4.   potato?   _____

5.   mosquito?   _____

C. Jack's parents live on a farm in the country. What does he see there?

1.   calf in the barn?   *There are many calves.* _____

2.   shelf on the wall?   _____

3. Is there only leaf on the tree? _____

4.   handkerchief in the drawer? _____

5.   loaf on the table?   _____

Check

Jack loses everything. Tell him where his things are.

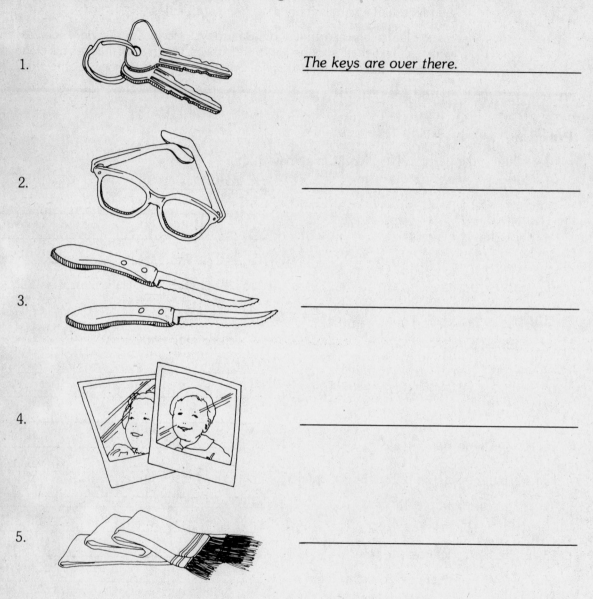

1. _____ *The keys are over there.* _____

2. _____ _____

3. _____ _____

4. _____ _____

5. _____ _____

4. Presentation   Common irregular plural nouns

child - children	aircraft - aircraft
foot - feet	deer - deer
goose - geese	fish - fish
man - men	sheep - sheep
mouse - mice	
ox - oxen	
tooth - teeth	
woman - women	

Nationalities ending in -ese

a Chinese	three Chinese
a Japanese	two Japanese
a Congolese	three Congolese

Compounds with man

a Frenchman	Frenchmen	a sportsman	sportsmen
an Englishman	Englishmen	a gentleman	gentlemen

Exceptions:	a German	two Germans
	a Roman	ten Romans

Practice

1.   sheep   *I saw many sheep there.*

2.   goose   _____

3.   mouse   _____

4. I saw a woman there.   _____

5.   child   _____

6.   Chinese   _____

7.   Frenchman   _____

8.   Swiss   _____

Check

A. Complete these sentences with the correct plural form.

1. Martha met many __*Japanese*__ in Tokyo. (Japanese)
2. She ate a lot of _____ while in Japan. (fish)
3. She had to use chopsticks instead of _____ and forks. (knife)
4. Martha had to have a dentist look a her _____ in Tokyo. (tooth)
5. Later, Martha visited her friends, Henri and Paul, who are two _____ from Paris. (French)
6. They both teach _____ in a local school. (child)
7. Martha was having a good time until she broke both _____ in an accident! (foot)
8. She was chasing _____ out of the barn, tripped and fell. (mouse)

B. Fill in *is* or *are* to complete the sentences.

1. The English __*are*__ very friendly people.
2. I don't know where my passport _____.
3. Does anyone know where the Italians _____?
4. The highways _____ very dangerous.
5. The Irish _____ very patriotic.
6. Martha's cat _____ sitting on the floor.
7. The children _____ playing in the yard.
8. The dog _____ running along with the children.

5. Presentation   **Restrictions of singular/plural nouns**

Some nouns are restricted to either singular or plural.

Singular

Joyce Brennan owns a travel agency in San Francisco. Her *income* is good. The *advice* and *information* she gives to her customers is valuable. She receives all the latest *news* about airline price changes and is very sure to tell her clients. She recently redecorated her office with new *furniture* that is very modern.

Plural

The *police* are investigating the scene of a crime. There has been a suspicious fire in a store on Jefferson Avenue. "The *ashes* are still hot and the *steps* are loose and very dangerous," called out Officer Brennan. He discovered some strange *glasses* and a pair of *scissors* near the door. What could that mean?

Use of plurals with parts of the body

After the investigation, the police officers washed their *faces* and *hands*. Many of the men had scraped their *knees* and bruised their *arms* on the loose stairs.

Practice

A. Is Joyce's income good or bad?   *Her income is good.* _____

   1. Is her furniture modern or antique?   _____

   2. Is her information important?   _____

   3. Is the news useful or useless?   _____

   4. Is the advice helpful?   _____

B. Are the police clever?   *The police are clever.* _____

   1. Are the stairs safe or unsafe?   _____

   2. Are the ashes cold or hot?   _____

   3. Are the scissors sharp?   _____

   4. Are the glasses on the floor?   _____

C. What did Officer Brennan and Joyce do . . . ?

1. . . . when they said good-bye?   *They waved their hands* _____

2. . . . when they said "no"?   *They shook their* _____

3. . . . before they ate dinner?   *They washed their* _____

4. . . . when they were excited?   *They waved their* _____

D. Complete the sentences using *is* or *are*.

1. The information about the fire __*is*__ confidential.

2. Joyce's business _____ profitable.

3. The police _____ investigating the case.

4. The stairs in the store _____ broken.

5. Joyce's advice _____ useful.

6. Her income _____ very high this year.

6. Presentation   Countable and uncountable nouns

Things you can count:	Things you cannot count (mass nouns):
boys, houses, mistakes	relaxation, knowledge, milk

Sometimes the same word can stand for a countable or an uncountable.

I'd like a cake.	Too much cake is bad for you.
I've had many nice experiences.	That secretary hasn't had much experience.
We have a lamb on our farm. (the animal)	I don't eat lamb. (the meat)

Certain expressions are used with some mass nouns to designate quantity.

a slice of bread	a lump of sugar	a piece of wood
some bread	some sugar	some wood

Check

Find the correct expressions using the following vocabulary. Some answers will be used more than once.

piece	glass	slice	lumps
cup	bit	bar	

Paula: Waiter! I'd like a ___*cup*___ of coffee. Is it possible to put six _____

of sugar in it? And, I'd also like a _____ of bread with jam, butter, mustard

and chocolate syrup on it, a _____ of cheese and a _____ of

mineral water!

Waiter: . . . a _____ of cheese, and a _____ of mineral water. Okay, but

may I give you a _____ of advice? That meal does not sound at all appetizing

and perhaps a bit unsettling to the stomach. May I suggest our hamburg special instead?

Paula: Thank you for that _____ of information, but I don't intend to *eat* all that food!

I'll be using it in my beauty bath. Add a _____ of soap to the order too!

7. Presentation   The possessive genitive

In the singular, the genitive is formed by adding apostrophe (') s.

Whose book is it? It is the boy's book.
Whose pen is it? It is the teacher's pen.

In the plural, the genitive is formed by adding apostrophe (') OR apostrophe + s ('s).

Plurals ending in -s:	the boy	the boys' bikes
	the ladies	the ladies' hats
Plurals *not* ending in -s:	the men	the men's room
	the children	the children's toys

Double usage (of/'s)

I didn't know he was one of your son's friends.
He's been a friend of my son's for many years.

of is used about objects *and* animals

Objects:
The color of the house is green, but the roof of the house is black. The name of the street is Jackson.

Animals:
The tail of the tiger was very long in comparison to the tail of my cat!

The *of* genitive is also used to differentiate between singular and plural and as above in double usage ('s/s' = no pronunciation difference).

the girls' father = the father of the girls
the girl's father = the father of the girl

Practice

A. Does Molly have a dog?   *Yes, this is Molly's dog.*

1. Does Tom have a stereo?   _____

2. Does Molly have a car?   _____

3. Does Tom have a radio?   _____

4. Does Molly have a house?   _____

B. How long is Molly's vacation? (week)   *She has a week's vacation.* _____

  1. How long is her trip? (day)   _____

  2. How long is her wait for the ferry? (an hour)   _____

  3. How much pay does she have to spend? (week)   _____

C. How long a vacation do her friends have? (four weeks)   *They have four weeks' vacation.* _____

  1. How long is their journey? (five days)   _____

  2. How long is their wait at the airport? (three hours)   _____

  3. How much pay do they have to spend? (two months)   _____

D. Do the Browns live in this house?   *No, that's the Browns' house.* _____

  1. Do the Garcias own this car?   _____

  2. Do the Wongs drive this truck?   _____

  3. Do the Newmans own that cat?   _____

  4. Do the Dunns rent that cottage?   _____

  5. Do the Changs own this house?   _____

E. What did Molly paint?   (bedroom door)   *She painted the door of the bedroom.* _____

  1.   (garage roof)   _____

  2.   (kitchen floor)   _____

  3. What did Molly paint? (house number)   _____

  4.   (desk leg)   _____

  5.   (table top)   _____

F. I didn't know Molly was one of your son's
    friends.

She's been a friend of my son's for years.

1. I didn't know he was one of your
    husband's friends.

_____

2. I didn't know Molly was one of your
    parents' friends.

_____

3. I didn't know Peter was one of your
    son's friends.

_____

4. I didn't know Molly was one of your
    wife's friends.

_____

G. Whose notebook is this?

It's Don's.

1. Whose house is that?

_____

2. Whose paper is this?

_____

3. Whose purse is this?

_____

4. Whose pen is that?

_____

5. Whose office is this?

_____

6. Whose wallet is that?

_____

Check

A. Answer the questions using 's, s' or *of*.

1. How much vacation does Molly have? (two weeks)

   Two weeks' vacation. _____

2. How late was the plane? (one hour/ delay)

   _____

3. What did they pay Molly for? (five days/ work)

   _____

4. What did Molly paint? (roof/house)

   _____

5. Whose book is that? (Molly)

   _____

6. Whose dog is that? (Hamptons)

   _____

B. Now rewrite these.

1. One of Molly's dogs.

   A dog of Molly's. _____

2. One of the Hamptons' neighbors.

   _____

3. Some of the teachers' books.

   _____

4. One of the American's friends.

   _____

5. One of Dr. Hampton's patients.

   _____

6. Some of the artists' paintings.

   _____

Part IV/Pronouns

1. Presentation   Personal pronouns

Singular		Plural	
Subject	Object	Subject	Object
I	me	we	us
you	you	you	you
he	him	they	them
she	her		
it	it		

Personal pronouns used after verbs/prepositions:

Subject	Verb + object	Preposition	Object
I	closed the door	behind	me.
You	took the racket	with	you.
We	threw the ball	at	them.
They	tossed the ball	to	us.
He	put the racket	beside	him.

Note the usage of object forms in everyday speech:

It's me.
Open the door. It's us!
It's him.

I is always a capital letter.

I am going to play tennis with Gloria this afternoon. I hope to win the game.

Practice

A. Is that Greg's racket?   _Yes, the racket belongs to him._

  1. Is that Gloria's ball?   _____

  2. Is that her tennis court?   _____

  3. Is that your bag?   _____

  4. Is that my watch?   _____

42

B. He cannot play alone.   *I will play with him.* _____

   1. I cannot play alone.   _____

   2. Gloria cannot play alone.   _____

   3. We cannot play alone.   _____

   4. They cannot play alone.   _____

C. Is Gloria in the yard?   *Yes, she is.* _____

   1. Is the racket in the bag?   _____

   2. Are the balls on the court?   _____

   3. Are the scores on the board?   _____

   4. Are you playing tennis today?   _____

D. Where is Gloria's racket?   *She took it with her.* _____

   1. Where is Mr. Shelton's whistle?   _____

   2. Where is Greg's bag?   _____

   3. Where is your jacket?   _____

   4. Where is my hat?   _____

   5. Where is the coach's ball?   _____

E. Greg is hungry.   *Give him something to eat!* _____

   1. Gloria is hungry.   _____

   2. The other players are hungry.   _____

   3. The cats are hungry.   _____

   4. The coach, Mr. Shelton, is hungry.   _____

   5. Greg and Gloria are hungry.

2. Presentation   Word order

If the indirect object comes after the direct object you must use *to*.

I gave a book to him. He gave a bouquet of flowers to her.
(verb + direct object + to + indirect object)

If the direct object comes after the indirect object, omit *to*.

I gave him a book. He gave her some flowers.
(verb + indirect object + direct object)

The indirect object normally comes first unless it is very long.

I gave the book to the boy in the red sweater and blue pants.

OR if you want to emphasize the indirect object.

I gave the book to him. (not her)

After the following verbs, the indirect object must come *after* the direct object.

	described	Harry		us.
	introduced	Cecile		me.
	suggested	the proposal		us.
She	announced	the news	to	the students.
	confided	the secret		them.
	said	the speech		the audience.
	proposed	the plan		them.

When the direct object is a pronoun, use *to* + the indirect object.

He gave it to me.

Practice

Give me the book.   *Give the book to me.*

1. Hand me the pen.   _____

2. Write me a letter.   _____

3. Sing him the song.   _____

4. Read us the story.   _____

5. Tell me the truth.   _____

3. Presentation   Reflexive pronouns

I	myself	we	ourselves
you	yourself	you	yourselves
he	himself	they	themselves
she	herself		
it	itself		
one	oneself		

Some verbs are more often used with reflexive pronouns: *hurt, enjoy, warm, cut, make, amuse* and *ask*.

I hurt *myself* when I went skiing last weekend. *You* really enjoyed *yourself* at all the parties you went to while I was out on the slopes! *Elaine* cut *herself* before she even put on her skis and *Brett* simply warmed *himself* by the fire all weekend long. I think that I am the only one who went skiing. *We* certainly did make *ourselves* at home at the ski lodge. *You* all amused *yourselves* quite well. The *owners* probably asked *themselves* why they ever rented the place to such a large and noisy crowd.

Reflexive pronouns are also used when the object and the subject are identical. They are also used as a means of emphasis.

Brett looked at *himself* in the mirror. He almost didn't recognize *himself*! Elaine lives by *herself*; she does all of her housework *herself* and still has time for all of her hobbies. She said so *herself*. The work *itself* isn't so difficult.

Reciprocal pronouns are used to express mutual action.

They helped each other and loved each other very much.

Practice

A. Can I help Elaine?   *She can do it herself.* _____

   1.   you?   _____

   2.   him?   _____

   3. Can I help them?   _____

   4.   Brett?   _____

   5.   her?   _____

B. What's the matter with him?   *He made a fool of himself!* _____

   1.   you?   _____

   2.   her?   _____

3. What's the matter with them?   _____

4.   Brett?   _____

5.   us?   _____

Check

A. Complete the dialogue with the correct words.

1. Elaine lives by ___herself___.

2. Really? I thought Brett lived with _____.

3. No, they haven't lived with _____ for several months.

4. Brett lives by _____ now, too.

5. Does he still want to live with _____?

6. Yes, but Elaine feels that she simply can't live with _____.

B. Use the correct forms (him-himself) or (her-herself).

1. Brett sat all alone by ___himself___ at the ski lodge.

2. He was feeling sorry for _____ all weekend.

3. Elaine seemed to be enjoying _____ too.

4. Brett was angry when he saw Richard with _____.

5. She had cut _____ foot earlier, but was still having a good time.

6. He wasn't enjoying _____.

7. He wanted Elaine to notice _____.

8. He kept telling _____ that he still loved Elaine.

C. Fill in the missing words where necessary.

1. Brett and Elaine once loved ___each other___ very much.

2. Elaine discovered that she couldn't live with Brett even though she loved _____.

3. Brett was much too self-centered _____.

4. He was always telling _____ how wonderful he was.

5. She wondered whether she should live by _____.

6. Elaine also wondered whether she could ever forget _____.

4. Presentation   Possessive adjectives and pronouns

	Adjectives			Pronouns
	my school.			mine.
	your book.			yours.
	his pencil.			his.
This is	her paper.		This is	hers.
	our teacher.			ours.
	your composition.			yours.
	their class.	it—its		theirs.

Possessive pronouns have the same form in the singular and plural.

Is this book yours? No, that book is mine. (singular)
Are these books yours? No, those books are mine. (plural)

Practice

A. Is this book yours?　　　　　　　　*Yes, it's my book.*

　　1.　　　　pen hers?

　　2.　　　　school theirs?

　　3. Is this composition his?

　　4.　　　　class ours?

　　5.　　　　pencil mine?

B. Is this your pen?　　　　　　　　　*Yes, it's mine.*

　　1.　　　　Diana's notebook?

　　2.　　　　Carlo's class?

　　3. Is this their school?

　　4.　　　　our book?

　　5.　　　　my paper?

C. This is my sister, Diana.　　　　*I didn't know she was a sister of yours!*

　　1.　　　　my friend, Frank.

　　2.　　　　our teacher, Mrs. Martin.

3. This is their cousin, Anthony.   _____

4.   her friend, Elinor.   _____

5.   Carlo's friend, Paul.   _____

Check

A. Insert the appropriate pronoun: *me, my, mine* or *myself*.

1. Frank is a very good friend of _____*mine*_____.

2. He has always been a good friend to _____.

3. He is _____ best friend.

4. Frank helps _____ fix my car.

5. I could never do it _____.

6. Frank tries to teach me car repair so that I can do it _____.

7. He knows that _____ car is always in need of repair.

8. He is the only friend of _____ who knows exactly how to do things right!

9. Frank comes to _____ for help with his Spanish lessons.

10. I am glad that he is _____ friend.

B. Fill in the correct form of the verb (is/are).

1. —Are these your shoes?

   —No, mine ___*are*___ red.

2. —Is this your hat?

   —No, mine _____ yellow.

3. —Why aren't you drinking your milk?

   —Mine _____ sour.

4. —Why aren't you wearing your shorts?

   —Mine _____ too big.

5. —Why don't you borrow Frank's glasses?

   —Because his _____ not the right kind.

6. —Why hasn't Anthony done his work?

   —Because his _____ too difficult.

5. Presentation   Possessive/definite article before nouns

Nouns denoting parts of the body, articles of dress, ornaments, etc. which belong to the subject of an active sentence are generally used with a possessive adjective.

Yesterday was a bad day. Robby hurt *his leg*. Brenda lost *her ring*. Robby shrugged *his shoulders* when Brenda asked him if he had seen *her ring*. Their mother shook *her head*. She knows that her children constantly lose *their things* . . . when they aren't getting hurt!

The definite article is often used in passive sentences.

Robby was bitten in *the leg* by a huge dog. He was given a shot in *the arm* at the hospital.

The definite article is also used when the reference is to the object.

Brenda looked *him* in *the face*. When Robby found her ring, she kissed *him* on *the forehead*.

There are, however, many exceptions to the above rule:

The doctors turned *him* over on *his back* and then they helped *him* to *his feet*.

Practice

A. What's the matter with Robby?

He hurt his leg. _____

1. What's the matter with Margaret?

_____

2. What's the matter with the children?

_____

3. What's the matter with the dog?

_____

B. Describe the actions listed below.

1. What do you do if you
   mean "yes"?   nod/head   *You nod your head.* _____

2. What do you do if you
   don't know the answer?   shrug/shoulders   _____

3. What do you do if you
   want to ask a question
   in class?   raise/hand   _____

4. What do you do if you
   mean "no"?   shake/head   _____

C. Fill in the missing words.

1. Have you hurt ____*your*____ leg?

2. Carol carried an umbrella under _____ arm.

3. Robby was hit on _____ head by a falling stone.

4. Brenda took him by _____ arm.

5. She sometimes walks in _____ sleep.

6. The dog bit Robby in _____ hand.

7. He put _____ hand in cold water.

8. Carol led him by _____ hand.

6. Presentation   ***Use of the pronoun it***

It is used as a "dummy" subject in expressions of weather, temperature, time and distance constructions with forms of the verb *to be*.

It is cold in Montreal in January. *It* usually snows at this time of the year. *It* is 22 degrees Fahrenheit there right now. *It* is freezing! *It* is fifteen miles to the airport from here. *It* is ten o'clock and my plane leaves at eleven o'clock.

It is used as a "dummy" subject when the real subject is an infinitive or a *that* clause.

It is difficult to understand the announcer. = To understand the announcer is difficult.
It is true that the plane is late. = That the plane is late is true.

*The forms with *it* are more common and considered correct usage.

It is sometimes used as a subject when certain verbs are followed by an adjective *and* an infinitive.

	is	
	appears	
It	seems	easy to do!
	sounds	
	looks	

Practice

A. What's the weather like?

It is raining.

 1.    It's snowing

2.    It's sunny

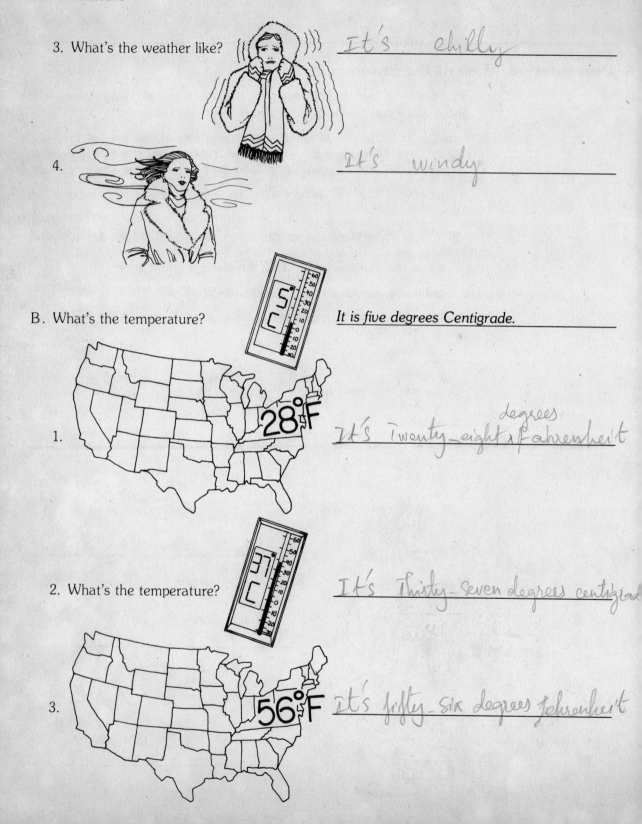

3. What's the weather like?   It's chilly

4.   It's windy

B. What's the temperature?   *It is five degrees Centigrade.*

1.   It's Twenty-eight degrees ∧ Fahrenheit

2. What's the temperature?   It's Thirty-seven degrees centigrad

3.   It's fifty-six degrees fahrenheit

C. What's the time?      *It is twenty-five past eight.*

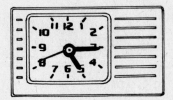

1.   It's quarter pass five

2.   it's Tewlere

3. What's the time?   it's half pass ten

4.   It's quarter to tewlere

5.   It's five minute pass Two

D. How far is it to New York?

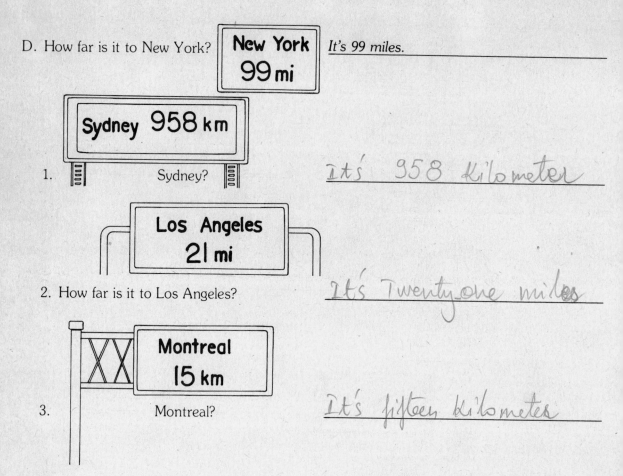

It's 99 miles.

1. Sydney?

It's 958 kilometer

2. How far is it to Los Angeles?

It's Twenty one miles

3. Montreal?

It's fifteen kilometer

E. Answer these any way you want.

Is it interesting or boring to learn English?

It is interesting/boring to learn English.

1. Is it simple or difficult to play the guitar?

It's difficult to play the guitar

2. Is it pleasant or unpleasant to wake up in the morning?

It's pleasant to wake up in the morning

3. Is it easy or hard to fly a plane?

It's easy to fly a plane

4. Is it usual or unusual to own five cars?

It's usual to own five cars

F. Have you found an apartment yet?

It seems difficult to find one.

1. Have you sold your car yet?

It seems difficult to sell car

2. Have you hired a maid yet?

It's seems difficult to hire a maid

3. Have you written your resume yet?

It's seems difficult to write resume

4. Have you gotten a job yet?

It's seems difficult to get a job

Presentation   Use of the pronoun *there*

There (sometimes called "preparatory *there*" because it prepares the subject) is used when the subject is a noun or a pronoun. The verb agrees in number with the subject.

There is a man coming upstairs. *There* aren't any pictures in the office. *There* isn't any doubt about it.

The preparatory *there* is often unnecessary.

There is a lamp on the table. / A lamp is on the table.
There is something beside the lamp. / Something is beside the lamp.
There are many other things on the table. / Many other things are on the table.

Practice

A. How many rooms are in the school?   26   *There are twenty-six rooms.* _____

   1. How many desks are in the class-
      room?   12   _____

   2. How many boxes are on the desk?   9   _____

   3. How many books are in the boxes?   4   _____

   4. How many papers are in the books?   16   _____

   5. How many students are in the class?   32   _____

B. Change the wording.

   1. Something is wrong.   *There is something wrong.* _____

   2. A lion is in the cage.   _____

   3. A lot is left.   _____

   4. A clown is in the tent.   _____

   5. A circus is going on.   _____

C. There were four thousand people there.   _There are usually thousands there._

1. There were ten dozen clowns there.

2. There were two hundred monkeys there.

3. There were five thousand balloons there.

4. There were six dozen lions there.

5. There were seven hundred children there.

Check

A. Answer the questions using *it* or *there*.

1. Where is the circus?   —_It_____ is at the stadium.

2. Can I buy a ticket at the stadium?   —Yes, _____ are many tickets available.

3. What time does the circus begin?   —_____ starts at one o'clock.

4. Where is the souvenir stand?   —_____ is at the corner.

5. How many balloons are on sale?   —_____ are hundreds on sale!

6. Now, where is your seat?   —_____ is near the stairway.

B. Fill in the blanks using *it* or *there*.

1. The circus was fun. __There_____ was so much to see!

2. _____ was exciting to watch the lion act.

3. _____ was so much tension in the air when the trainer put his head in the lion's mouth.

4. _____ ended at five o'clock.

5. _____ looks as though I will be able to see the circus again in New York.

6. _____ will probably be some new acts in the show by then.

8. Presentation Demonstrative pronouns and adjectives

Demonstratives are used in order to point out things.

Pronouns	Adjectives
This is my magazine.	*This* article is interesting.
That is your newspaper.	*That* column is well written.
These are my textbooks.	*These* editions are new.
Those are my albums.	*Those* records are quite good.

To denote comparison or selection, *this* one and *that* one may be used as pronouns instead of *this* and *that*, but only after countables.

This magazine is better than *that* one. *This* tea is sweeter than *that*.

Some expressions using *this*, *that*, *these* and *those*:

Please do it like *this*. I know best; *that* is why I am the boss. *That* will do for now. . . . Stop! *That* is it.

I got up at six *this* morning so that I could help you *this* afternoon. I'm planning to go out *this* evening and celebrate my friend, Cheryl's, birthday. She will be thirty *this* year! She's going to Brazil *this* summer so I won't be able to see her for quite a while. She was in Mexico *this* time last year. She travels a lot *these* days. It's not like it was when she was a student. In *those* days Cheryl could barely make ends meet.

Practice

A. Is this your newspaper?

No, that is my newspaper!

Are those your shoes?

No, these are my shoes.

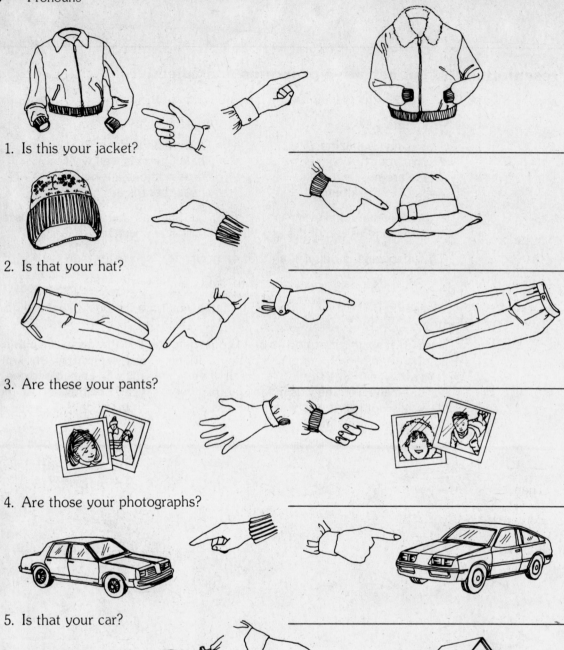

1. Is this your jacket? _____

2. Is that your hat? _____

3. Are these your pants? _____

4. Are those your photographs? _____

5. Is that your car? _____

6. Is this your house? _____

B. This book is very interesting. *This book is more interesting than that one.*

1. This car is very expensive. _____

2. That chair is very comfortable. _____

3. This picture is very beautiful. _____

4. That hotel is very expensive. _____

5. This dictionary is very useful. _____

Check

Fill in the blanks using *this*, *that*, *these*, and *those*.

1. When did you get up ____*this*____ morning?

2. Six o'clock. We'll have to work hard _____ afternoon.

3. You're going out with Cheryl _____ evening, aren't you?

4. Do you remember _____ night last spring when we all went out to eat?

5. _____ was a nice time.

6. In _____ times, it didn't cost much for a huge meal like the one we had.

7. It seems as though _____ was a long time ago, even though it's been only a year.

8. It really is less expensive to eat at home _____ days.

9. _____ is right.

10. Then, _____ is it! I'll cook dinner for Cheryl tonight. Do you want to come?

11. _____ will be the day I eat your cooking!

12. And _____ is the last time I'll invite you!

9. Presentation   Interrogatives

Who refers to people: *Whose* = possessive

Who is that man?   *Whose* father is that?
Who lives in this house?   *Whose* house is it?
Who have you given it to?   *Whose* is this?

(*Whom* as an object form is seldom used.)

Whom did you meet?

Which = a choice   *What* = explanation or query

Which sweater do you like?   *What* happened to your arm?
Which do you want?   *What* do you want?

Interrogatives in indirect speech:

	who had seen the accident.
	what had happened.
The police officer asked	which car was ours.
	whose car was damaged.

Check

A. Fill in the blanks with *who, whose, which* or *what.*

1. ___Who___ was in the car?

2. _____ car is it?

3. _____ street were you on?

4. _____ time did the accident take place?

5. _____ kind of car hit yours?

6. _____ was driving?

7. _____ way was the other car going?

8. _____ turn was it to go?

9. _____ kind of driver are you?

10. _____ insurance company will be responsible for the charges?

11. _____ color was the traffic light?

12. _____ way were you going?

13. _____ was the weather like?

14. _____ wants to go to the hospital?

B. Who saw the accident?   _I don't know who saw the accident._

   1. What happened?   _____

   2. Which bridge collapsed?   _____

   3. Who told the police?   _____

   4. What stopped the train?   _____

   5. Whose car hit the pole?   _____

C. Paul lives in that house.   _Who lives in that house?_

   1. Rick is going to help us.   _____

   2. I have seen the king.   _____

   3. I have given it to my son.   _____

   4. I'm working for Jones and Co.   _____

   5. Pamela is coming to see us.   _____

D. I have never seen those books before.   _I wonder whose they are._

   1. I have never seen these children before.   _____

   2. I have never seen this car before.   _____

   3. I have never seen those clothes before.   _____

   4. I have never seen that dog before.   _____

   5. I have never seen these shoes before.   _____

10. Presentation   Defining and nondefining relative clauses

Defining	The fishermen who are good sailors go out in any weather. (*only* good sailors go out, not all the fishermen)
Nondefining	The fishermen, who are good sailors, go out in any weather. (not one definite group of fishermen, all of them)

Nondefining relative clauses are not common in spoken English. However, if they are used, remember the following:

They must have commas.	My uncle, who is from Puerto Rico, is coming to the party.
Do not omit the relative pronoun.	My father, who(m) you have met, is coming as well.
Prepositions governing the relative are usually placed at the beginning of the clause.	The boat, about which you have heard a lot of stories, will be docked at the harbor.

The relative pronoun is often omitted in defining clauses if:

—it is the object	The man (who/m) you saw was my uncle.
—if the preposition which governs it comes at the end of the clause.	The boat (which) you gave me a ride in was great!

That cannot be used in nondefining clauses.

Nondefining	Defining
Dick's boat, which is in the harbor, is greatly admired.	The boat that is in the harbor is not mine.

Check

Defining or Nondefining? Write *D* or *N* next to the sentence.

1. __D__ The man who helped you was my uncle.

2. _____ The woman who is in the boat, is my aunt.

3. _____ My uncle, Simon, whom everyone loves, is a good fisherman.

4. _____ People who have never fished don't know what a great sport it is!

5. _____ The boat that is in the harbor is quite large.

6. _____ The big boat, which belongs to my uncle, is wonderful.

7. _____ My aunt, who is afraid of sailing, still goes on the boat with my uncle.

8. _____ The fishermen who work with my uncle are very skillful.

9. _____ The fishermen you saw at the pier are friendly.

10. _____ The boat, which cost a lot of money, was stolen.

11. _____ The police officer, who was very busy, did not stop.

12. _____ The thief who stole the boat was very clever.

B. Fill in the blanks with *who, whose, which* or *that* where necessary.

1. The story ___*that*___ you told me was not true.

2. The boys _____ father was ill have come for a job.

3. My sons, _____ are all very good sailors, have gone to sea.

4. I bought the book _____ you told me about.

5. I met the man _____ got the job.

6. The President, _____ has not been well for a long time, is better now.

7. The Queen, _____ is loved by everyone, was greeted by loud cheers.

8. The Concorde, _____ was a fine machine, was a financial fiasco.

9. My home, _____ was only a tent, was paradise to me.

10. The house _____ you built fell down.

11. Presentation   Relative pronouns

Who/that are used in reference to people:

Todd is the man		is moving to New York.
Todd is the musician	who	played the guitar.
Those are the people		were in the audience.

Whose is used in reference to possession:

Do you know		instruments those are?
Todd is the one	whose	guitar was stolen.
I wonder		fault it was.

Which/That is used in reference to objects and animals:

The guitar		was stolen is expensive.
Are these the instruments	which/that	were in the club?
The police found the guitar		was stolen.

That is also used after superlatives:

It was the finest guitar that I have ever seen.
The guitar was the most expensive one that was in the store.
Todd is the best guitarist that many people have ever heard!

That is used after *all*, *everything* and *much*.

This is *all that* is left in the club. Tell me *everything that* has happened.

After the emphatic construction *it is*, *it was*, etc., the relative pronoun, *that*, is often omitted.

It must have been about this time (*that*) it happened. It was here (*that*) the crime took place.

Practice

A. Who saw the robbery?   *I'd like to know who saw it!*

1. Which guitar was stolen?   _____

2. Who told the police?   _____

3. What happened?   _____

4. Whose guitar was stolen?   _____

B. Do you want this album?   best   _That album is the best one that there is._

   1.   guitar?   most expensive   _____

   2.   stereo   nicest   _____

   3. Do you want this
      instrument?   most difficult   _____

   4.   case?   heaviest   _____

   5.   music?   easiest   _____

C. Give me everything you have.   _I've given you everything that I have._

   1. Did he lose everything he owned?   _____

   2. Tell me everything you know.   _____

   3. Did you believe everything he said?   _____

   4. Tell me everything you heard.   _____

   5. Show me everything you have.   _____

D. He knows everything.   _There's not much that he doesn't know._

   1. He can afford everything.   _____

   2. She can play anything.   _____

   3. They sell everything.   _____

   4. They check everything.   _____

E. Did you say Gary stole the
   money?   boy   _Gary's the boy who stole the money._

   1. Did you say Mr. Mackey
      takes your children to
      school?   neighbor   _____

   3. Did you say Miss Oakes
      teaches them French?   teacher   _____

   3. Did you say that Patrick
      didn't pay?   guest   _____

4. Did you say Henry made all
   those mistakes?   student   _____

5. Did you say Mary won first
   prize?   pupil   _____

F. Are all the other planes full?   *This is the only plane that's not full.*

   1.   cars dirty?   _____

   2. Are all the other shops closed?   _____

   3.   toys broken?   _____

   4.   pictures taken?   _____

G. Fill in the blanks with *who, whose, which,* or *that.*

   1. The musicians __*who*__ work with Todd wanted to perform tonight.

   2. But, the guitar _____ was Todd's pride and joy was stolen.

   3. _____ guitar was it?

   4. The show _____ was scheduled was cancelled by the manager.

   5. The manager, in _____ club the robbery took place, might give Todd some money
      to replace his guitar.

   6. Large crowds come to the concerts _____ Todd performs.

   7. It is worth it to the manager _____ runs the club to buy Todd a new instrument.

   8. _____ night will the rescheduled concert take place?

   9. Eventually the police will find the thief _____ stole everything.

   10. Perhaps everything _____ was taken will be recovered.

2. Presentation   *Some* and *any* and compounds

Some or *some* + *compounds* is used chiefly in affirmative sentences:

some	someone	something	somehow
somebody	some one	somewhat	somewhere

I would like some sugar in my tea.
(Would you like some milk as well? = politeness usage)

Any or *any* + *compounds* is used chiefly in negative sentences, questions or conditional clauses:

any	anyone	anything	anywhere
anybody	any one	anyhow	

I don't want any, thank you anyhow.
You don't know anyone at the party, do you?
If anyone calls, say that I'm out.

Some or *any* can be used in comparative statements or to make specific distinctions.

She is taller than *some* of my friends.	She is taller than *any* of my friends.
He works better than *some* other pupils.	He works better than *any* other pupils.
Some of the students can do it.	*Any* of the students can do it.

Practice

A. Is there any milk in the kitchen?   <u>*Yes, there is some milk.*</u>

1. Is there any butter on
   the plate?   _____

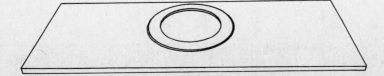

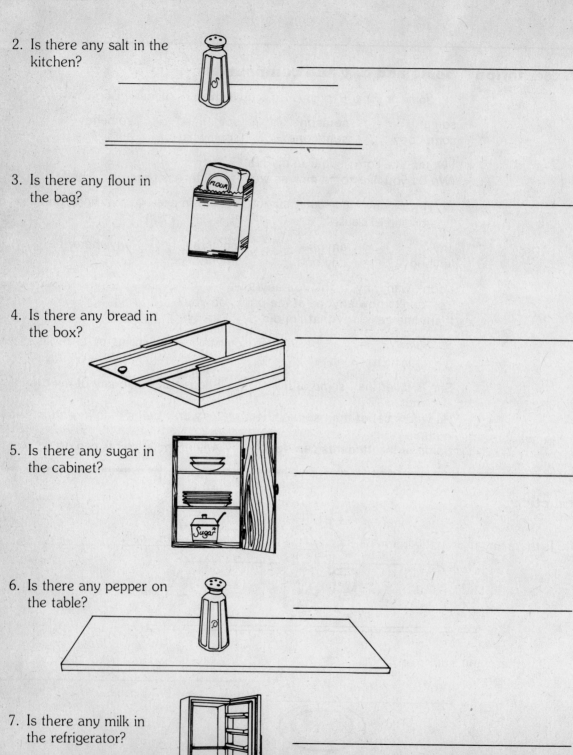

2. Is there any salt in the
   kitchen?

3. Is there any flour in
   the bag?

4. Is there any bread in
   the box?

5. Is there any sugar in
   the cabinet?

6. Is there any pepper on
   the table?

7. Is there any milk in
   the refrigerator?

B. Are there any apples on the table?

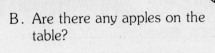

No, there aren't any apples.

1. Are there any eggs in the carton?

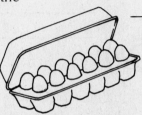

_____

2. Are there any bananas on the table?

_____

3. Are there any napkins on the chair?

_____

4. Are there any oranges in the bag?

_____

5. Are there any grapes in the dish?

_____

C. Are there any knives and forks
on the table?

There are some knives but there aren't any forks.

1. Are there any cups and
saucers on the table?

_____

_____

2. Are there any glasses and
bottles on the table?

_____

_____

3. Is there any wine and beer
on the table?

_____

_____

4. Is there any bread and
butter on the table?

_____

_____

D. Is there anybody outside the bank?

There is somebody inside the bank.

1. Is there anything behind the desk?

_____

2. Is there anyone under the tree?

_____

3. Is there something under the table?

_____

4. Is there anything behind the bush?

_____

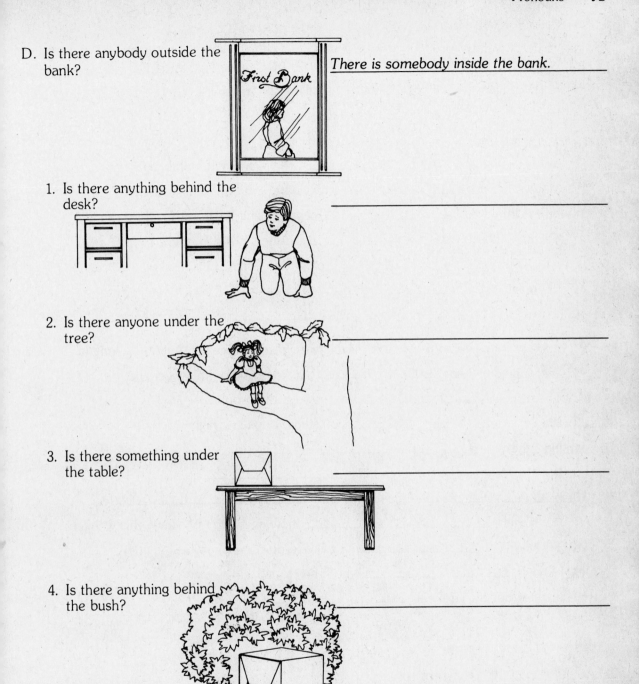

E. Fill in the blanks with *some, any, something, anything, someone, anyone, anywhere,* or *somehow.*

1. I cannot find _____ *any* _____ milk in the refrigerator.

2. Is there _____ in the oven?

3. There are _____ cookies!

4. There might be _____ else to eat in the kitchen.

5. Maybe _____ could prepare you a meal.

6. I don't know _____ who is willing to do it though.

7. Tell me if there is _____ coffee in the kitchen.

8. I would like _____ tea if there isn't _____ coffee.

9. There isn't _____ to go to eat.

10. _____ I must find _____ for dinner!

F. Fill in the blanks with *some, any, someplace, anyplace, someone, anyone* or *anything.*

1. We wanted to find _____ to go skiing this weekend.

2. There isn't _____ snow on the ground.

3. We expected _____ snow to fall last night.

4. Now there isn't _____ to go to ski.

5. We like to go skiing and then have _____ tea.

6. _____ might like to have _____ coffee.

7. But if there isn't _____ snow, we won't be skiing this weekend.

8. There isn't _____ I like to do more than ski.

9. I know _____ who hates to ski.

10. I never thought I'd meet _____ like that.

3. Presentation   *Any* in affirmative sentences

Any (and compounds) is used in seemingly affirmative sentences whose basic idea is actually negative.

He did it without *anyone* (anybody) seeing him. = No one saw that he did it.

Jean drives better than *any* of her friends. = None of Jean's friends drive as well as she does.

I don't think that *anything* can surprise me any longer. = I think that nothing can surprise me any longer.

I have hardly *any* money. = I have almost no money.

Any (and compounds) is used in affirmative sentences in the sense of no matter who (which, what, where). In that case, it is generally stressed.

Any day will suit me.
I must find a box. *Any* box will do.
Anything may happen.

You can mail a letter at *any* post office.
Anyone can do what I did!
You can sleep *anywhere* you like.

Check

Fill in the blanks with *some*, *any*, or compounds.

1. __*Some*__ children don't like ice cream but most do.

2. _____ tickets you can't sell may be returned.

3. Don't you have _____ news for me? Or am I mistaken?

4. _____ you can do I can do better.

5. Don't worry! Call me at _____ time, day or night.

6. I'm expecting _____, please call me.

7. _____ of my friends have not met you.

8. I don't have _____ to do.

9. Be prepared for the worst. _____ might happen.

10. These things are very popular. You can buy them at _____ store!

14. Presentation   Usage of *one* and *ones*

Manuel is wearing a blue sock and a red *one*. His jacket is old, but he just bought a new *one*. He left the other *one* at home. He would like to buy some green pants and some blue *ones*. He has some brown *ones* but he doesn't like them.

One - ones are not used with nouns that do not form a plural.

There was no hot water, only cold. (water)
Manuel never has bad luck, only good. (luck)

One - ones are not used after cardinal numbers.

He needs three ties but he has only two. (ties)
Manuel has one car but his father has three. (cars)

One - ones are not used directly after "own" or "these/those."

Manuel doesn't need to use that car. He owns his own.
He does need to borrow those pants and those ties.

Check

Fill in the blanks with *one* or *ones* when necessary.

1. Manuel bought a new car _____.

2. It is not a new _____.

3. In fact, it is a rather old _____.

4. Manuel doesn't like the new _____ because they are too expensive.

5. He only needs one car, but his father has three _____.

6. Manuel hasn't had bad luck with his car, only good _____.

7. He likes blue jeans, especially the _____ with big pockets.

8. He needs to buy a green shirt; he wants a plaid _____.

9. He bought these red pants and those brown _____.

10. Manuel doesn't need to borrow a belt; he has his own _____.

Part V/Adjectives

1. Presentation **Comparison of adjectives**

Adjectives of one syllable

Sandy is tall.   Kasim is taller.   Kim is the tallest.

Kasim is very tall.   Kim is the very tallest.
Kasim is taller than Sandy.   Kim is much taller than Sandy.
Kim is even taller than Kasim.

Adjective of two syllables ending in -y, -er, -ow, -le.

pretty	prettier	the prettiest
clever	cleverer	the cleverest
narrow	narrower	the narrowest
noble	nobler	the noblest

Spelling: Consonant + y becomes: -ier
-iest

| heavy | heavier | the heaviest |
| happy | happier | the happiest |

Final consonant doubled (after single, stressed vowel)

big	bigger	the biggest
fat	fatter	the fattest
red	redder	the reddest

Practice

A. Follow the pattern and fill in the correct forms.

—This ball is *big*.

—But this ball is *bigger*.

—This is the *biggest* of all!

    _____big_____   _____bigger_____   _____biggest_____

1. This cow is fat.   _____ _____ _____
2. This pig is thin.   _____ _____ _____
3. This field is flat.   _____ _____ _____
4. This story is sad.   _____ _____ _____
5. This room is hot.   _____ _____ _____

B. Kasim is very young   his cousin   *But his cousin is even younger.*

1. Sandy is strong   her sister   _____
2. Kim's skis are long.   Alice   _____
3. Mr. Stone's car is large.   Mrs. Hill   _____
4. Sandy's face is red.   Kim   _____
5. The trip to London is long.   New York   _____

C. Kim is taller than all of her friends.   *Yes, she's the tallest girl.*

1. Miss Garcia is kinder than the other teachers.   _____
2. Sandy is slimmer than everybody else.   _____
3. This test is harder than any other one.   _____
4. This store is cheaper than the others.   _____
5. This journey is longer than any other.   _____

D. Follow this pattern and fill in the correct forms.

—This bag is *heavy*.

—Is it *heavier* than my bag?

—Yes, this is the *heaviest* bag of all.

heavy	*heavier*	*heaviest*
1. This idea is silly.		
2. This room is chilly.		
3. This dog is friendly.		
4. This orange is juicy.		
5. This puzzle is easy.		

E. Follow the pattern with the sentences below.

—Jack is very tall.

—Yes, he's much taller than Tom.

—I think he's even taller than Peter.

—No, he's not as tall as Peter.

1. My room is very hot.   Maria's/Ramon's

— _____
— _____
— _____

2. My car was very cheap.   Sue's/Jeff's

— _____
— _____
— _____

3. My sister is very cute.   Jessica/Sean

— _____
— _____
— _____

2. Presentation   More/most comparisons

Most adjectives of two or more syllables use this form:

useful	more useful	the most useful
careful	more careful	the most careful
interesting	more interesting	the most interesting
dangerous	more dangerous	the most dangerous
worn out	more worn out	the most worn out

Jean is intelligent.
Jean is very intelligent.
Jean is more intelligent than her sister.
Jean is much more intelligent than her brother.
Jean is even more intelligent than her mother.
Jean is as intelligent as her father.

Irregular comparison

good	better	the best
well	better	the best
bad	worse	the worst
ill	worse	the worst
little	less	the least
many	more	the most
much	more	the most

Sarah went to a very *good* restaurant in the city but Tim claims that he went to a *better* one and had *the best* steak in the world there. Then Sarah went to the movies. She has seen many *bad* films but this particular film was the *worst* one she has ever seen. It was *worse* than the film she had seen the week before.

Practice

A. Isn't Tim foolish?   his brother   <u>*Yes, but his brother is more foolish.*</u>

1. Isn't mother careful?   her sister   _____

2. Isn't this book interesting? Juan's book   _____

3. Isn't this chair comfortable? that sofa   _____

4. Isn't the principal worn out? that teacher   _____

B. Follow the pattern with the sentences below.

—Kevin is not a *helpful* person.

—His brother is even *less helpful.*

—I thought Kevin was the *least helpful* person in the world.

1. Hiro is not a careful driver.   father

— _____

— _____

2. Mr. Gunther is not a brilliant teacher.   Miss Hamton

— _____

— _____

3. Ken's term paper is not interesting.   Pam

— _____

— _____

4. Jane's idea is not useful.   Allan

— _____

— _____

5. Dudley is not a serious person.   Steve

— _____

— _____

C. Is the weather good?   *It's better than yesterday.* _____

   1. Is she well?   _____

   2. Is your cold bad?   _____

   3. Is he still ill?   _____

   4. Are there many problems?   _____

   5. Is there much tea left?   _____

3. Presentation   Irregular comparisons

near	nearer	nearest/next
old	older/elder[1]	oldest/eldest
late	later/latter[2]	latest/last

These adjectives have irregular forms in either the comparative or superlative.

Louise lives *near* Woodside Park. Ryan lives even *nearer* to the park. Jim thought that he lived the *nearest* until he found out that MaryBeth lived *next* to the park.

[1]The forms *elder/eldest* are sometimes used with close relatives. My *elder* brother . . . his *eldest* daughter.

[2]*Latter* means the last mentioned. He likes tea and coffee, but I prefer the *latter*.

Check

Use the above words in these sentences.

1. I live in an apartment _____*near*_____ the museum.

2. Jeremy is _____ than his friend, Ricardo.

3. I found a watch and a ring. The _____ is very valuable.

4. Alicia loves her _____ son more than any of her other twelve children.

5. Have you heard the _____ news about the hurricane?

6. I'm busy now. Can we play _____?

7. Where is the _____ restaurant?

8. It's _____. It is time to go home.

9. The bus stop on Highland Avenue is _____ than the one on Essex Street.

10. I will help you _____ time we meet.

Part VI/Adverbs

1. Presentation

Formation of adverbs

Adverb + verb	He runs quickly.
Adverb + adjective	She is extremely beautiful.
Adverb + adverb	They worked extremely quickly.

Adverbs are usually formed by adding *-ly* to an adjective.

kind	kindly	quick	quickly	beautiful	beautifully
bad	badly	slow	slowly	useful	usefully
important	importantly	careful	carefully	wonderful	wonderfully

Spelling of adverbs

consonant + *y*		*-le* becomes *-ly*	
Adjective	Adverb	Adjective	Adverb
happy	happily	possible	possibly
easy	easily	comfortable	comfortably
heavy	heavily	probable	probably
dirty	dirtily	idle	idly
angry	angrily	able	ably

Exception: shy   shyly

Adjectives and adverbs with the same form

Adjective	Adverb
I subscribe to a *daily* newspaper.	He calls *daily*.
I get *hourly* reports.	The bus arrives *hourly*.
It is a *weekly* magazine.	They pay *weekly*.
It is a *monthly* journal.	I am paid *monthly*.
He is a *fair* player.	Play *fair*.
This is a *hard* job.	Work *hard*.
He came by the *late* train.	He came *late*.
They took the *early* train.	She left *early*.

Practice

A. I think he's a careful worker.   *Yes, he works carefully.*

   1.   he's a beautiful singer.   _____

   2.   she's a fantastic dancer.   _____

   3. I think they are brilliant actors.   _____

   4.   he's a careless driver.   _____

   5.   she's a quick worker.   _____

B. Select the appropriate words to fill in the blanks.

happy	easy	angry
happily	easily	angrily

   1. The teacher was ___*angry*___ because the students did their work.

   2. The homework was _____ .

   3. Sometimes the teacher speaks _____ to the class because they haven't done their work.

   4. But this was _____ the least difficult assignment yet!

   5. The students _____ completed the work.

   6. So, the teacher wasn't _____ at all!

C. Was he polite when he answered you?   *He answered politely.*

   1. Was he brave when he fought the lion?   _____

   2. Was she strange when she talked to you?   _____

   3. Were they fierce when they attacked?   _____

   4. Was your grandmother comfortable when she rested?   _____

D. Does he report to the police daily?   *He makes daily reports.*

   1. Does he visit the doctor weekly?   _____

   2. Does she call the hospital hourly?   _____

   3. Does he forecast the weather monthly?   _____

   4. Does the manager write orders daily?   _____

Check

A. Underline the appropriate word.

1. Bob will (probable/<u>probably</u>) arrive at eight o'clock.

2. You will feel (comfortable/comfortably) with him.

3. Bob acts more (polite/politely) than most people.

4. It is (possible/possibly) that Bob will bring a friend with him.

5. Bob gets along with people most (easy/easily).

6. He makes friends (quick/quickly).

7. You will (probable/probably) gain a new friend!

8. Bob fits in most (comfortable/comfortably) with any group of people.

B. Is he a good player?   *No, he plays badly!* _____

1. Is he a good singer?   _____

2. Is she a good speaker?   _____

3. Are they good painters?   _____

4. Are they good dancers?   _____

5. Are they good actors?   _____

C. Underline the appropriate word.

1. Mr. Johnson works (<u>hard</u>/hardly).

2. He is a (fair/fairly) employer.

3. (Late/Lately) he has been working until seven o'clock every night.

4. Then, Mr. Johnson goes (direct/directly) home.

5. He is a (fair/fairly) fast driver.

6. He takes a (direct/directly) route home.

7. Mr. Johnson doesn't really enjoy working (late/lately) every night.

8. He has (hard/hardly) any spare time anymore.

2. Presentation   Regular comparison of adverbs

-ly adverbs

easily	more easily	most easily
quickly	more quickly	most quickly
comfortably	more comfortably	most comfortably
politely	more politely	most politely

I always drive *carefully*. You must drive more *carefully*. Mother always drives most *carefully*.

Single syllable adverbs + early

soon	sooner	soonest
hard	harder	hardest
early	earlier	earliest

I'll see you *soon*. I get up *earlier* than anybody in my house. I work the *hardest*.

Irregular comparison of adverbs

badly	worse	worst
well	better	best
little	less	least
much	more	most
far	further/farther	furthest/farthest

I played *badly*, but you played worse. I worked a *little* and you worked *less*, but she worked *least* of all.

Practice

A. Answer the questions.

Bill can run a hundred yards in 13 seconds.
Herb can run a hundred yards in 14 seconds.
Steffy can run a hundred yards in 15 seconds.
Libby can run a hundred yards in 14 seconds.

1. Can Bill run as fast as Libby, or can he run faster than her?
   Bill can run faster than Libby.

2. Can Bill run as fast as Herb, or can he run faster than him?

3. Can Herb run as fast as Libby, or can he run faster than her?

4. Can Steffy run as fast as Libby, or can she run faster than her?

_____

5. Can Libby run as fast as Bill, or can she run faster than him?

_____

6. Can Steffy run as fast as Herb, or can she run faster than him?

_____

7. Who is the fastest runner?

_____

8. Who is the slowest runner?

_____

B. Will you be home soon?   *I'll be home sooner than you think.*

  1. Will he work hard?   _____

  2. Will they be home late?   _____

  3. Will she arrive early?   _____

  4. Will we fly high?   _____

  5. Will he finish soon?   _____

C. Follow this form and fill in the correct forms.

—You played *badly*, didn't you?

—I've never played *worse*.

—I know, Toby said you'd played *worst* of all.

badly	*worse*	*worst*
1. You worked very little, didn't you?		
2. You played well, didn't you?		
3. You threw the ball far, didn't you?		
4. You danced so much, didn't you?		

3. Presentation   Verbs that take adjectives

The following verbs take adjectives rather than adverbs:

smell
Is lunch ready yet? It
smells good.
I don't want that egg. It
smells bad.

taste
This fish tastes bad.
The cake tastes
wonderful.

be
Be careful.
I am happy.

become
The children became
tired.
I became very sad.

keep
Keep calm.
Keep quiet.

grew
She grew nervous.

look
They looked sincere.
Look happy!

feel
I feel sick.
She feels bad.

turn
He turned green with
envy.

seem
The dogs seem hungry.
She seems tired.

sound
That sounds interesting.
The music sounds
beautiful.

Practice

A. Underline the appropriate word.

1. Alfredo is (<u>happy</u>/happily).

2. He feels (glad/gladly) because he just got a job.

3. Alfredo went to a restaurant to celebrate his (good/goodly) fortune.

4. Everything smelled (wonderful/wonderfully).

5. The waiters were (kind/kindly).

6. The fish seemed (fresh/freshly).

7. The bread tasted (delicious/deliciously).

8. The desserts looked (marvelous/marvelously) but Alfredo couldn't eat any more.

9. The meal was (expensive/expensively) but Alfredo didn't care.

10. His new job sounds so (important/importantly).

11. He wonders if this job will be (good/better) than his last one.

12. Alfredo felt (unhappy/unhappily) at that job.

B. Choose the appropriate response from the possibilities below.

	work			longer.
	days	is		easier.
Yes, the	winters		getting	colder.
	summers	are		wetter.
	weather			drier.
	climate			harder.
				milder.

1. It's dark early now.   _The days are getting shorter._

2. It's light now.   _____

3. It's dry.   _____

4. It's a cold winter.   _____

5. It's a warm winter.   _____

6. It's an easy exercise.   _____

C. Underline the appropriate word.

1. Glenn tried to keep (<u>calm</u>/calmly).

2. He grew more and more (nervous/nervously) as the minutes ticked by.

3. He was (tire/tired).

4. He felt (hungry/hungrily).

5. His wife seemed (happy/happily).

6. She looked (content/contentedly).

7. Their new baby was (beautiful/beautifully).

8. Glenn felt (great/greatly).

4. Presentation   Word Order — Adverbs of time

1. Adverbs of time are usually placed between the subject and the main verb.
2. They can be placed between the auxiliary verb and the main verb.
3. With "to be" they are usually placed after the verb in statements, after "not" in negatives and after the subject in interrogatives.

I	sometimes	have	a cold.
I	always	go	there.
I	seldom	went	there.
	never		

I have		gone	there.
I don't	often	go	there.
Do you		go	there?

He is not			in a hurry.
I am	always		in a hurry.
Are you			in a hurry?

Practice

A. What about you?

1. Do you always sleep well?   *No, I never sleep well.*

2. Do you always get up early?   _____

3. Did you always do your homework at school?   _____

4. Have you always spent your vacation in Spain?   _____

5. Will he always make the same mistake?   _____

6. Can you always do as you like?   _____

B. Is he busy?   always   *He is always busy.* _____
    1. Are they in a hurry?   never   _____
    2. Is she asleep?   often   _____
    3. Are you angry?   always   _____
    4. Is he tired?   seldom   _____
    5. Are you disappointed?   often   _____

C. Now change the word order.
    1. Is he sad?   always   *He always is.* _____
    2. Are they working?   never   _____
    3. Are they tired?   seldom   _____
    4. Is he disappointed?   never   _____
    5. Are you angry?   always   _____

D. Answer the questions in your own way.

always	usually	seldom
soon	never	often

1. When will you leave school?   *I will leave school soon.* _____
2. Have you often been to England?   _____
3. How often do you smoke?   _____
4. Do you sometimes get up late?   _____
5. Do you usually drive to school?   _____

Part VII/Verbs

1. Presentation   Classification of Verbs

English verbs may be:

1. *Auxiliary* (= *helping*) *verbs*, help to form the tenses and moods of other verbs.
   (a) *have*: helping to form the perfect and pluperfect tenses
       be: helping to form the passive voice and the continuous tenses
       do: helping to form certain questions and negative sentences
   (b) The Modal auxiliaries are usually followed by the simple form of the verb.
       can, could, may, might, must, shall, should, will, would, ought, used
       and in some cases *dare* and *need*.

2. *Main Verbs.* (Full verbs)
   (a) *Regular verbs*: verbs that form the past tense and the past participle by
       adding -*ed* to the simple form: walk - walked - walked
   (b) *Irregular verbs*: verbs that form the past tense and the past participle
       in some other way: speak - spoke - spoken

Full verbs have the following simple forms and tenses.

1. *The infinitive*
   to go, to come, to sing

2. *The present tense*
   | I wait | I go | I sing |
   | He waits | He goes | He sings |

   The present tense has the same forms as the simple form except in the third
   person singular, which is formed by adding -*s* or -*es* to the simple form.

3. *The past tense*
   The past tense is the same in all persons and is formed:
   (a) with the regular verbs by adding -*ed* to the simple form.
       he waited, he walked, he kissed
   (b) with the irregular verbs in some other way:
       he wrote, he went

4. *The imperative* (command)
   The imperative always has the same form as the infinitive (without *to*)
   Turn. Play. Go.

5. *The present participle*
   is formed by adding -*ing* to the simple form
   waiting, going, being, singing

6. *The past particple*
   (a) With regular verbs it has the same form as the past tense.
       waited, walked, kissed
   (b) With irregular verbs in some other way:
       written, gone, sung

2. Presentation   The verb *to be*

Present		Past	Present perfect	Past perfect	Future	Present participle
I	am	was	have been		shall be	
You	are	were			will be	
He						
She	is	was	has been	had been	will be	being
It						
We						
You	are	were	have been		shall be	
They						
					will be	

Not is placed after the first verb.

I was not unhappy.
We were not there.
David had not been to Paris.
I shall not be at home there.
Pablo will not be happy.

The verb *to be* is used in the imperative.

Be quiet!   Don't be silly.
Be a good kid!   Don't be lazy.
Be careful.   Don't be unhappy.

Questions: Note that the word order for questions changes. The first verb is put before the subject in order to pose a question.

You are playing.   you (are) playing.   Are you playing?

He was working.   he (was) working.   Was he working?

She has been working.   she (has) been working.   Has she been working?

Practice

A. I am late for school.   I   *Am I late too?*

   1. Juan is here.   David   _____

   2. David is hungry.   Juan   _____

   3. They are tired.   their parents _____

4. They were in Paris.   you   _____

5. Francis was there.   Rodney   _____

B. Answer these questions positively and negatively.

1. Are you ill?   *Yes, I am.* _____

                         No, I'm not. _____

2. Was he busy?   _____

                         _____

3. Were they angry?   _____

                         _____

4. Is she unhappy?   _____

                         _____

5. Have they been asleep?   _____

                         _____

6. Have you been to college?   _____

                         _____

7. Is he impatient?   _____

                         _____

C. They have been to Paris.   London   *Have they been to London?*

1. They have been to see Francis.

                         Rodney   _____

2. Pablo will be hungry when he   thirsty
   comes.
                         _____

3. Francis was eating his egg.   bread   _____

4. He had been playing with his   friend
   brother.
                         _____

5. Rodney would be surprised to   happy
   hear that.
                         _____

D. David is unhappy.   Juan   _Juan is not unhappy._____

   1. His brother is ill.   sister   _____

   2. Rodney and Francis   Paula and Pablo   _____
      are on vacation.

   3. Juan was in the car.   David   _____

   4. They were hungry.   their friends   _____

   5. David was late.   Juan   _____

E. Paula has been ill.   her brother   _I hope her brother has not been ill.____

   1. Paula should have   Pablo   _____
      been in Madrid.

   2. The children were   dogs   _____
      playing in the pool.

   3. Pablo will be late.   Paula   _____

   4. He will be tired.   his father   _____

F. Have you been to Brazil?   you   _Haven't you been to Brazil yet?_____

   1. Is your brother at school?   your sister   _____

   2. Were you happy yesterday?   you   _____

   3. Was Paula at home?   Juan   _____

   4. Has your father helped you?   mother   _____

   5. Are you hungry?   you   _____

3. Presentation   Form of *to be* + infinitive

This form indicates that something will happen according to a timetable, program or previous agreement.

My aunt Shirley from Hartford was to visit us yesterday. We were to pick her up at the airport but she decided to drive here today instead. She was to leave Hartford at noon and arrive here by five o'clock. We plan to take her to the theater. The play is to start at eight o'clock. It is to end at ten o'clock.

Practice

A. When was your aunt to visit?   yesterday   _____

   1. Where were you to pick her up?   airport   _____

   2. When was your aunt to leave Hartford?   noon   _____

   3. When is she to arrive here?   five   _____

   4. When is the show to start?   eight   _____

   5. When is the play to end?   ten   _____

B. Complete these dialogues.

—Uncle Albert is late.

—When was the plane to land?

__*It was to land at twelve o'clock.*__

   1. —Mother is late.

      —When was she to arrive at the airport?

—_____

   2. —The plane should have arrived by noon.

      —When was it to arrive?

—_____

   3. —The play hasn't begun yet.

      —When was it to begin?

—_____

---

4. Presentation   Negative imperatives, questions and statements with the verb *do*

A form of the verb *do* and *not* is used to make negative imperatives.

Go!	Do not go!	Don't go!
Come here!	Do not come here!	Don't come here!

A form of the verb *do* and *not* is used to make negative questions.

Don't you like Keith? Doesn't Mary like you? Didn't we meet you there before?

A form of the verb *do* and *not* is used to make negative statements.

I do	I
You do (don't)	You
H(she) does (doesn't) like spinach.	H(she) did not eat lunch. (didn't)
We do	We
You (don't)	You
They	They

Practice

A. Keith and Mary sing at parties.   *But they don't sing well.*

   1. We play guitars.   _____

   2. They dance all night.   _____

   3. You harmonize with the boys.   _____

   4. I sing often.   _____

B. Keith acts in plays.   *But he doesn't act well.*

   1. He drives a sports car.   _____

   2. Mary plays tennis.   _____

   3. She sleeps a lot.   _____

   4. Keith works every day.   _____

C. They played baseball yesterday.   *But they didn't play long.*

1. Mary waited for Keith.   _____

2. They washed their clothes last night.   _____

3. Keith worked hard.   _____

4. He played guitar at the party.   _____

D. Fill in the blanks with *don't, doesn't* or *didn't*.

1. *Didn't* _____ Keith and Mary live in Chicago last year?

2. He _____ like living in big cities, so he and Mary moved.

3. Mary _____ enjoy the city either.

4. She _____ like their apartment in Chicago.

5. They _____ regret moving to this small town.

6. Keith _____ find a job for nearly five months.

7. _____ Mary work at the college now?

8. However, she _____ have to work there anymore.

9. Yet she _____ like staying home all day.

10. _____ I hear that she may get a part-time job?

E. Follow the patterns.

1. I am not fond of dancing.   *Don't you dance at all?*

2. Keith painted the house.   *Didn't he paint it himself?*

3. Mary seldom watches TV.   *Doesn't she ever watch it?*

4. Keith repaired my car.   _____

5. She rarely waits for him.   _____

6. They seldom go to bed early.   _____

7. Keith never plays the stereo.   _____

8. Mary seldom stays home.   _____

5. Presentation   Questions with the verb *do*

Do-does-did are used in forming questions.

What does he want?	He wants fish.
Does he want meat?	No, he wants fish.
What do they want?	They want coffee.
Do they want tea?	No, they want coffee.
What did she want?	She wanted a skirt.
Did she want jeans?	No, she wanted a skirt.

Do the Riveras live on your street? Doesn't Stuart know them? Does Stuart see them often? Don't the Riveras have a young daughter named Leslie?

Practice

A. Martin plays golf before breakfast.   *Does he really play golf before breakfast?*

1. He smokes fifty cigarettes a day.   _____

2. Judie speaks fifteen languages.   _____

3. She washes her car every day.   _____

4. The cat catches three mice a day.   _____

B. Mother mailed a letter.   *Did she mail my letter too?*

1. Steve washed my car.   _____

2. My sister painted my bicycle.   _____

3. Judie washed my shirt.   _____

4. The children repaired my radio.   _____

C. I had fish for breakfast this morning.   *Do you have fish every morning?*

1. We had wine with lunch today.   _____

2. They had yogurt for dessert.   _____

3. I had eggs and bacon for breakfast.   _____

4. We had chicken for lunch yesterday.   _____

D. Stuart taught French.   Spanish   *Did Stuart teach Spanish, too?* _____

   1. He spoke Italian.   English   _____

   2. Stuart met the teachers.   principal   _____

   3. He saw his friend, Leslie.   Gordon   _____

   4. They bought hamburgers.   ice cream   _____

   5. They ate lunch together.   dinner   _____

E. Leslie had a salad for lunch.   *Does she always have salad?* _____

   1. Stuart had cereal for breakfast.   _____

   2. Gordon had fish for lunch.   _____

   3. Leslie had steak for dinner.   _____

   4. Stuart had pork roast on Sunday.   _____

   5. Gordon had juice for breakfast.

F. What are they saying?

6. Presentation   Question patterns

Do-Does-Did are *not* used when the subject of the clause is unknown. Instead, question words like *who, whose, what, which,* and *how* are used to ask the question. The subject of the clause is a question word.

Who lives here?	I live here.
What bit you?	A dog bit me.
Which book is yours?	This is mine.
Whose book cost $25?	Susan's cost $25.
How many people live here?	Four live here.

Do-Does-Did plus *not* are used in negative questions even if the subject is a question word.

Who didn't come to your party?
How many children don't have their lunches with them?
Which house doesn't have a garage?

Practice

A. Somebody said you were ill.   *Who said I was ill?*

   1. Somebody paid a thousand dollars for it.   _____

   2. Somebody broke the window.   _____

   3. Somebody made a mistake.   _____

   4. Somebody won a prize.   _____

B. Something fell out of the window.   *What fell out of the window?*

   1. Something hit my foot.   _____

   2. Something exploded. ·   _____

   3. Something dropped out of your pocket.   _____

   4. Something broke the vase.   _____

C. One of the boys hit the girl.   *Which boy hit the girl?*

   1. One of the books belonged to Eddie.   _____

   2. One of the cars crashed into the bank.   _____

3. One of the dogs bit the mail carrier.   _____

4. One of the girls asked about you.   _____

D. I want to know who likes chocolate.   *You'd better ask who does like chocolate.*

   1. I want to know how many smoke.   _____

   2. I want to know what hurts you.   _____

   3. I want to know who wants to come.   _____

   4. I want to know whose mother works.   _____

E. Some of them didn't pay.   how many   *I'd like to know how many didn't pay.*

   1. Somebody doesn't like   who
      me.   _____

   2. Something makes a   what
      noise.   _____

   3. Somebody's dog   whose
      doesn't sleep at night.   _____

   4. One of the boys didn't   which
      go.   _____

Check

Fill in *do*, *does*, or *did* where necessary.

1. What _____ happened?

2. Who _____ you meet last night?

3. How many people _____ you know here?

4. How many students _____ fail this test each year?

5. Who _____ typed the letter?

6. Which _____ article was published?

7. Which one _____ you write?

8. What _____ you see at the theater?

9. How many pets _____ you own?

10. Which hat _____ you buy yesterday?

7. Presentation   The verb *have*

	Present	Past	Perfect	Past Perfect
I You	have		have had	
He She It	has	had	has had	had had
We You They	have		have had	

Practice

A. Fill in the blanks with *have* or *has*.

1. My sister ____has____ a very quick temper.

2. The Crawfords _____ a very nice garden.

3. Janet's dog _____ fleas.

4. John and Kathy _____ a lot in common.

5. My cousin _____ a beautiful smile.

6. Tom _____ a new sailboat.

B. Fill in the blanks with *have*, *has* or *had*.

1. My uncle did not ____have____ a chance in the finals.

2. The local store does not _____ any bread left.

3. Yesterday we did not _____ any supper.

4. If I _____ known you were coming I'd _____ baked a cake.

5. They _____ no clothes in their suitcases.

6. They've _____ all the chances they'll get.

7. By this time tomorrow I'll _____ already arrived in Japan.

8. I _____ a strange dream last night.

8. Presentation   Regular verbs

		Present	Past	Present perfect (has/have)	Past perfect (had)	Future
1st person s.	I			played		play
1st person p.	We	play		have	played	shall
2nd person s./p.	You	wash		washed had		wash
3rd person s. {	He		played		washed	
	She	plays	washed	played		play
	It	washes		has		will
3rd person p.	They			washed		wash

Simple present tense is used in these situations:

—habitual, customary actions: Leah walks to the store every morning.
—permanent truths: Honesty is a good attribute.
—series of actions: He goes to the window, looks out, screams and collapses.
—with adverbs such as: always, often, sometimes, usually
—with adverbial phrases such as: everyday, once a week, twice a night
—with time clauses such as: whenever, every time that . . .

Pronunciation

If the verb ends in any of the following sounds:
    [s] [dz] [z] [s] [ts]
then -es is added in the third person singular

pu*sh* - pushes   *sneeze* - sneezes   wat*ch* - watches
ju*dge* - judges   pa*ss* - passes

Present -s is voiced after voiced sounds and is voiceless after voiceless sounds.
     -es is pronounced after such words as kisses, buzzes, washes, judges

Spelling

Verbs that end in consonant plus -y take the ending -ies in the third person singular present tense.

Please carry this box! Dennis carries his books to school.

But a final -y after a vowel does not change the ending.

I play guitar and she plays flute. They played many different instruments.

Practice

A. Describe the characters' days.

1. Rafael	2. Leah	3. Dennis	4. Janis
7:30 bus/school 2:30	10:10 car/work 6:30	9:45 train/work 5:00	8:20 plane/New York 4:00

1. *Rafael leaves home at 7:30. He takes the bus to school. He comes home at 2:30.*

2. _____

3. _____

4. _____

B. What does Leah sell
   every day?   books   *Leah sells books every day.*

   1.   wear   suit   _____

   2.   eat   salads   _____

   3. What does Leah drive
      every day?   van   _____

   4.   read   newspaper   _____

C. Who does Rafael talk
   to every day?   his father   *Rafael talks to his father every day.*

   1. What does Rafael eat
      every day?   cereal   _____

   2. What does Rafael play
      every day?   basketball   _____

   3. What does Rafael walk
      every day?   his dog   _____

   4. What does Rafael ride
      every day?   bicycle   _____

D. Answer the questions.

Dennis makes tea. First, he fills the teapot with water. Then he turns on the stove. He takes the teapot. He warms it with hot water. He puts a teabag into the pot. He pours milk into the cup. He pours the tea. He adds the sugar. He stirs the tea with a spoon. He drinks the tea.

1. What does Dennis fill?

   Dennis fills the teapot with water.

2. What does he turn on?

3. What does he do to the teapot?

4. How much tea does he put in?

5. What does he pour into the cup?

6. What does he pour after the milk?

7. What does he add?

8. What does he stir with?

Check

A. Underline the correct verb.

1. Rafael (swim/<u>swims</u>) in the lake every summer.

2. He (hurry/hurries) to the lake every day.

3. Rafael and his brother (play/plays) on the beach every afternoon.

4. They (live/lives) nearby.

5. Sometimes Rafael (help/helps) his mother with the housework.

6. He usually (wash/washes) the dishes.

7. He (watch/watches) TV after dinner every night.

8. Rafael and his brother often (ride/rides) their bikes to the beach.

B. What does Janis wash
every day?   hair   *Janis washes her hair.*

  1. What does Janis brush
    every day?   dog   _____

  2. What does Janis
    sometimes miss?   plane   _____

  3. Who does Janis usually
    kiss?   husband   _____

  4. What does Janis always
    watch?   TV   _____

C. What does Dennis fly
every day?   jet   *Dennis flies a jet.*

  1. What does he often
    carry?   maps   _____

  2. What does he usually
    worry about?   weather   _____

  3. What does Dennis
    sometimes study?   schedules   _____

  4. Where does Dennis
    usually hurry to?   airport   _____

D. Where does Dennis stay?   Hilton   *He stays at the Hilton.* _____

   1. What does he play?   golf   _____

   2. When does he pray?   Sunday   _____

   3. Who does he annoy?   mother   _____

   4. What does he enjoy?   flying   _____

E. What do they play?   *They play tennis.* _____

   1. What does Janis like?   _____

   2. Where do they sit?   _____

   3. What do you study?   _____

   4. When does she leave?   _____

5. How does Leah travel?   _____

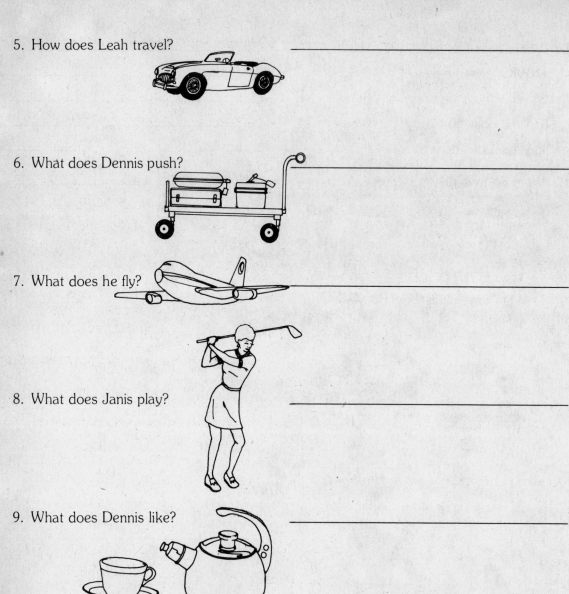

6. What does Dennis push?   _____

7. What does he fly?   _____

8. What does Janis play?   _____

9. What does Dennis like?   _____

10. Where do they live?   _____

9. Presentation   **Simple Past**

Simple past tense is used to describe an action that has already taken place.

The teacher *talked* to Gail about her grades yesterday. She *asked* her several questions about her study habits.

The regular ending of simple past verbs is *-ed*.

Gail *wanted* to get good grades. She *visited* the library often and *looked* for good books.

When a simple verb ends with *-e*, it is only necessary to add *-d* to form the simple past.

Gail *changed* her habits. She even *moved* closer to school.

When a simple verb ends with *-y* and is preceded by a consonant, the *-y* becomes *-i* and *-ed* is added to form the simple past tense.

Gail *hurried* home from school every day and *studied* very hard.

When a one syllable verb ends in a consonant but is preceded by a single stressed vowel, the end consonant is doubled before *-ed*.

Gail *stopped* watching TV so much. She *planned* to become a doctor one day.

Practice

A. Fill in the correct form of the verb.

1. Gail (talk) ___talked___ to her teacher for advice.

2. Her friend, Robin, (help) _____ her with her homework.

3. She (ask) _____ her many questions.

4. Gail (type) _____ several letters.

B. Fill in these blanks now.

1. Gail (want) ___wanted___ to graduate from college with honors.

2. She (visit) _____ the library nearly every day.

3. Gail (graduate) _____ in May.

4. Robin (wait) _____ for her.

C. Fill in the blanks with the correct form of the verb.

1. Robin (tutor) __*tutored*__ at the college last year.

2. Gail (listen) _____ to Robin.

3. She (receive) _____ a diploma.

4. Gail (move) _____ to St. Louis.

D. What did Gail study?   medicine   *Gail studied medicine.* _____

1. What did she try to find?   job   _____

2. What did she carry?   briefcase   _____

3. Where did Gail hurry?   hospital   _____

4. Why did Gail cry?   sad   _____

E. Fill in the blanks with the correct form of the verb.

1. Gail (stop) __*stopped*__ at Union Hospital.

2. She (drop) _____ by to see her old friend, Benjamin.

3. Gail (admit) _____ that she needed a job.

4. It (occur) _____ to Benjamin that there was a job available in his department.

5. He (plan) _____ to ask his supervisor if Gail could interview for the position.

Check

A. Fill in the correct form of the verb.

1. Gail (study) __*studied*__ to become a doctor.

2. She (move) _____ to St. Louis.

3. She (hope) _____ to find a job there.

4. Gail (visit) _____ her friend, Benjamin.

5. She (live) _____ near him many years ago.

6. Benjamin (plan) _____ find a job for Gail.

7. He (want) _____ to work with her.

8. He (try) _____ to get her a job at the hospital.

9. Gail (apply) _____ for the position and got it.

10. Gail (thank) _____ Benjamin.

11. He (ask) _____ her out for dinner.

12. Gail (reply) _____ "Yes."

13. They (stop) _____ at a very expensive restaurant.

14. They both (order) _____ wonderful meals.

15. Within two years, Gail and Benjamin (marry) _____ each other.

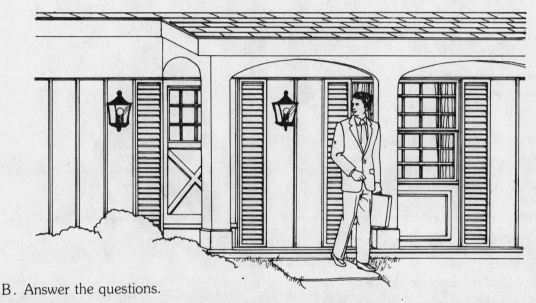

B. Answer the questions.

At a quarter past eight Benjamin opened his front door and walked down the garden path. He opened the garden gate and waved good-bye to the baby. Then he closed the gate and walked along the sidewalk. He stopped at the bus stop and looked at his watch. It was twenty past eight. He waited for five minutes. The bus arrived at twenty-five past eight.

Benjamin reached the hospital at five to nine and unlocked the door to his office. The nurse arrived five minutes later. They started work at nine. First of all, Benjamin examined some patients and the nurse helped him out.

They worked all morning and stopped at twelve for lunch. Then they worked all afternoon and tried to finish early because Benjamin wanted to play golf. At three o'clock he hurried out to catch the bus to the golf course.

1. When did Benjamin open his front door?

   Benjamin opened his front door at quarter past eight.

2. What did he do when he opened the garden gate?

_____

3. Where did he stop?

_____

4. What did he look at?

_____

5. How long did he wait?

_____

6. When did the bus arrive?

_____

7. When did Benjamin reach the hospital?

_____

8. When did the nurse arrive?

_____

9. What did Benjamin do first of all?

_____

10. What did the nurse do?

_____

11. When did they stop for lunch?

_____

12. How long did they work?

_____

13. What did they try to do?

_____

14. What did Benjamin want to do?

_____

15. What did he do at three o'clock?

_____

10. Presentation   **Simple future**

Simple future tense is used to describe an action that is going to take place in the future. It can be formed in three different ways:

—A form of the verb *be* + *going to* + simple verb

Michael *is going to drive* to the beach.

—*Will* + simple verb

Michael *will swim* in the ocean.

—*is* + *about to* + simple verb

Michael *is about to leave* for the beach now.

Practice

A. Michael is going to Europe next month. What will he do there?

1. sightsee

   He is going to sightsee.

2. buy new clothes

   _____

3. visit his relatives.

   _____

4. drive to France

   _____

5. go mountain climbing in the Alps

   _____

6. swim in the Mediterranean Sea

   _____

B. What is Michael about to do?

1. buy a train ticket

   Michael is about to buy a train ticket.

2. meet his friend, Enid

   _____

3. hike in the mountains

   _____

4. see his cousin in Paris

   _____

C. What will Michael do tomorrow?

1. pay his hotel bill

   He will pay his hotel bill.

2. kiss Enid good-bye

   _____

3. take the train to Paris

   _____

4. call his parents

   _____

Check

What about you?

1. What are you going to do this summer?

   I am going to _____

2. What will you do tomorrow?

   _____

3. What are you planning to do next year?

   _____

1. Presentation   Alphabetical list of irregular verbs

If you don't know the meaning of each verb, translate it and make a note of it here.

awake	_____	awoke	awaked, awoke
be	_____	was	been
bear	_____	bore	borne, born
beat	_____	beat	beaten
become	_____	became	become
begin	_____	began	begun
bend	_____	bent	bent
bind	_____	bound	bound
bite	_____	bit	bitten
blow	_____	blew	blown
break	_____	broke	broken
bring	_____	brought	brought
build	_____	built	built
burn	_____	burnt, burned	burnt, burned
buy	_____	bought	bought
catch	_____	caught	caught
choose	_____	chose	chosen
come	_____	came	come
cost	_____	cost	cost
creep	_____	crept	crept
cut	_____	cut	cut
deal	_____	dealt	dealt
dig	_____	dug	dug
do	_____	did	done
draw	_____	drew	drawn
dream	_____	dreamt, dreamed	dreamt, dreamed
drink	_____	drank	drunk
drive	_____	drove	driven
eat	_____	ate	eaten
fall	_____	fell	fallen
feel	_____	felt	felt
fight	_____	fought	fought
find	_____	found	found
fly	_____	flew	flown
forget	_____	forgot	forgotten
freeze	_____	froze	frozen

get	_____	got	got/gotten
give	_____	gave	given
go	_____	went	gone
grow	_____	grew	grown
hang	_____	hung, hanged	hung, hanged
have	_____	had	had
hear	_____	heard	heard
hide	_____	hid	hidden
hit	_____	hit	hit
hold	_____	held	held
hurt	_____	hurt	hurt
know	_____	knew	known
lay	_____	laid	laid
lead	_____	led	led
learn	_____	learnt, learned	learnt, learned
leave	_____	left	left
lend	_____	lent	lent
let	_____	let	let
lie	_____	lay	lain
light	_____	lit, lighted	lit, lighted
lose	_____	lost	lost
make	_____	made	made
mean	_____	meant	meant
meet	_____	met	met
pay	_____	paid	paid
put	_____	put	put
read	_____	read	read
ring	_____	rang	rung
rise	_____	rose	risen
run	_____	ran	run
say	_____	said	said
see	_____	saw	seen
seek	_____	sought	sought
sell	_____	sold	sold
send	_____	sent	sent
set	_____	set	set
shake	_____	shook	shaken
shoot	_____	shot	shot
show	_____	showed	shown
shut	_____	shut	shut
sing	_____	sang	sung

sink	_____	sank	sunk
sit	_____	sat	sat
sleep	_____	slept	slept
smell	_____	smelt, smelled	smelt, smelled
speak	_____	spoke	spoken
spell	_____	spelt, spelled	spelt, spelled
spend	_____	spent	spent
stand	_____	stood	stood
steal	_____	stole	stolen
swear	_____	swore	sworn
swim	_____	swam	swum
take	_____	took	taken
teach	_____	taught	taught
tell	_____	told	told
think	_____	thought	thought
throw	_____	threw	thrown
wake	_____	woke, waked	waked, woken
wear	_____	wore	worn
weep	_____	wept	wept
win	_____	won	won
write	_____	wrote	written

12. Presentation   Irregular verbs

Verbs that remain the same in present, past and past participle

bet	cut	read*	split
bid	hit	rid	spread
broadcast(ed)	hurt	set	thrust
burst	let	shed	upset
cast	put	shut	wed
cost	quit	slit	wet

*Spelling is the same; pronunciation differs.

Verbs in which the end consonant changes in the past tense:

Present	Past	Participle**
bend	bent	bent
build	built	built
burn	burnt, burned	burnt, burned
dwell	dwelt	dwelt
learn	learnt, learned	learnt, learned
lend	lent	lent
send	sent	sent
smell	smelt, smelled	smelt, smelled
spell	spelt, spelled	spelt, spelled
spend	spent	spent
spill	spilt, spilled	spilt, spilled
spoil	spoilt, spoiled	spoilt, spoiled

**Participle form is the same as the past form.

Verbs in which vowels *and* consonants change. Similar sounds but watch the spelling!

Present	Past	Participle*
bring	brought	brought
buy	bought	bought
catch	caught	caught
fight	fought	fought
seek	sought	sought
teach	taught	taught
think	thought	thought

Verbs in which the vowel sound changes [i] as in i̱t to [ə] as in a̱bout.

Simple	Past	Simple	Past
cling	clung	stick	stuck
dig	dug	sting	stung
fling	flung	string	strung
sling	slung	swing	swung

slink	slunk	win	won
spin	spun	wring	wrung

Verbs in which the vowel sound changes [e] as in <u>ea</u>sy to [e] as in b<u>e</u>d.

Simple	Past	Simple	Past
bleed	bled	lead	led
breed	bred	lean	leant
creep	crept	leap	leapt
deal	dealt	leave	left
dream	dreamt	mean	meant
feed	fed	meet	met
feel	felt	read	read
flee	fled	sleep	slept
keep	kept	sweep	swept
kneel	knelt	weep	wept

Verbs in which the vowel sound changes [ai] to [au]:

Simple	Past	Simple	Past
bind	bound	grind	ground
find	found	wind	wound

Other irregular forms:

Simple	Past	Simple	Past
lay	laid	have	had
pay	paid	make	made

Verbs in which the vowel sound changes in the past tense.

Simple	Past	Participle
become	became	become
come	came	come
hang	hung	hung
hear	heard	heard
hold	held	held
light	lit	lit
lose	lost	lost
overcome	overcame	overcome
run	ran	run
say	said	said
shoot	shot	shot
sit	sat	sat
slide	slid	slid
stand	stood	stood
strike	struck	struck
tell	told	told
understand	understood	understood

Verbs with vowel changes and different past participle forms:

Simple	Past	Participle
begin	began	begun
drink	drank	drunk
swim	swam	swum
ring	rang	rung
shrink	shrank	shrunk
sing	sang	sung
sink	sank	sunk
spring	sprang	sprung
stink	stank	stunk

Verbs with past participles ending with -n:

Simple	Past	Participle
arise	arose	arisen
awake	awoke	awaken
be	was/were	been
bear	bore	born/borne
beat	beat	beaten
bite	bit	bitten
blow	blew	blown
break	broke	broken
choose	chose	chosen
do	did	done
draw	drew	drawn
drive	drove	driven
eat	ate	eaten
fall	fell	fallen
fly	flew	flown
forget	forgot	forgotten
forgive	forgave	forgiven
forsake	forsook	forsaken
forbid	forbade	forbidden
freeze	froze	frozen
get	got	gotten
give	gave	given
go	went	gone
grow	grew	grown
hide	hid	hidden
know	knew	known
lie	lay	lain
ride	rode	ridden
rise	rose	risen

see	saw	seen
sew	sewed	sewn
shake	shook	shaken
shear	sheared	shorn
show	showed	shown
slay	slew	slain

Simple	Past	Participle
sow	sowed	sown
speak	spoke	spoken
steal	stole	stolen
stride	strode	stridden
strive	strove	striven
swear	swore	sworn
swell	swelled	swollen
take	took	taken
tear	tore	torn
throw	threw	thrown
tread	trod	trodden
wear	wore	worn
weave	wove	woven
write	wrote	written

Practice

A. Answer these questions.

1. Did you think the restaurant was good
   or bad?   *I thought the restaurant was bad.*
   _____

2. Did the waiter bring you tea or coffee?   _____

3. Did you buy lunch or dinner?   _____

4. Did you teach your friend how to order
   in Italian or Chinese?   _____

B. How did you feel
   yesterday?   sad   *I felt sad yesterday.*
   _____

1. What did you dream
   about?   robbery   _____

2. Where did you keep
   the necklace?   closet   _____

3. How did the robber
   leave?   through window   _____

4. Where did the track
   lead?   into woods   _____

C. Fill in the blanks with the appropriate form of the verb.

1. Sonia (lead) _____*led*_____ the children around the farm.

2. She showed them where the horses are (breed) _____.

3. They watched as the horses (leap) _____ over the hurdles.

4. The children had (read) _____ about farms in school.

5. They met the farm hand who (sweep) _____ the barn.

6. Sonia (mean) _____ to show them the dairy too, but there wasn't enough time.

7. They did (meet) _____ the owner of the farm though.

8. The children all (feel) _____ happy at the end of the tour.

D. Answer these questions any way you like.

1. Did the child dig a hole?   *Yes, the child dug a hole.* _____

2. Did the baby swing her arms or legs?   _____

3. Did a bee or wasp sting him?   _____

4. Did the team win the game?   _____

E. What did you bid at the auction? $300   *I bid $300 at the auction.* _____

1. How much did the painting cost? $800   _____

2. Where did you put the painting?   bedroom   _____

3. When did Peter quit his job?   yesterday   _____

4. What did he hurt?   arm   _____

F. Fill in the blanks with the appropriate form of the verb.

1. The athletes (swim) __*swam*_____ across the English Channel.

2. The crowd (begin) _____ to arrive at noon.

3. The chorus (sing) _____ songs to entertain the crowd.

4. Many people had (drink) _____ too much.

5. They (ring) _____ the bell to start the race.

G. What did they send to the architect?   telegram   *They sent the architect a telegram.* _____

1. What did he build?   hotel   _____

2. What did they lend him?   money   _____

3. What did they spend? $5 million   _____

4. What did the architect learn?   business   _____

H. Fill in the blanks with the appropriate form of the verb.

1. Ruth (make) __*made*_____ some cookies for dessert.

2. First, she (find) _____ the electric mixer.

3. Then, she (grind) _____ the nuts.

4. Ruth (have) _____ to bake the cookies for 20 minutes.

5. When the cookies were done, Ruth (lay) _____ them on the counter to cool.

I. Did Julia come to class yesterday?   *Julia came to class yesterday.*_____

1. Did Julia understand the chemistry
   lesson?   _____

2. Did she hear the homework
   assignment?   _____

3. Did Damien tell her about it?   _____

4. Did he say when the paper is due?   _____

Check

A. Use the past form of the verb.

1. Kate (meet) ____*met*_____ her boyfriend, Andy, at school.

2. He (speak) _____ to her in class.

3. They (drink) _____ coffee in the cafeteria.

4. Andy (bring) _____ Kate flowers.

5. They (begin) _____ to see each other every day.

6. Kate (dream) _____ about Andy.

7. She (feel) _____ good when she was with him.

8. Andy (leave) _____ to go to college.

9. He (keep) _____ in touch with Kate.

10. They (send) _____ each other letters.

B. Use the correct form of the following verbs:

feed	string	get	hear
ring	catch	eat	find

1. The children ___strung___ the lights on the tree.
2. They _____ their gifts under it in the morning.
3. They had _____ a nice present for their parents.
4. Their mother _____ the family later in the day.
5. They all _____ a lot of food.
6. Suddenly the telephone _____.
7. They _____ from their relatives in Mexico.
8. They _____ up on all the news.

C. Last year we went to Brazil for our vacation. We went by boat. The boat left at three o'clock on Monday afternoon. It took us two days to get to Brazil. The weather was fairly good. We bathed every day and lay on the beach until late at night. Then we went back to the hotel where we were staying. There was a dance every night—but sometimes we went for a walk along the beach or looked at the shops and clubs in the town. Our vacation lasted for two weeks and then it was time for us to go home again. And when we got home . . . it was raining.

Now write about *your* vacation.

1. Where did you go last year?

   Last year I went to . . . _____

2. How did you go?

   _____

3. When did you leave?

   _____

4. How long did it take you to get there?

   _____

5. What was the weather like?

   _____

6. What did you do every day?

   _____

7. What did you do in the evening?

_____

8. Where were you staying?

_____

9. How long did the vacation last?

_____

10. What was the weather like when you got home?

_____

D. Make questions.

1.	*What did he cut?*	He cut	a piece of string.
2.	*What did he give her?*	He gave	her some flowers.
3.	_____	He said	thanks.
4.	_____	He took	a taxi.
5.	_____	He wrote	a postcard.
6.	_____	He found	nothing.
7.	_____	He told	her the truth.
8.	_____	He thought	that it was very good.
9.	_____	He caught	a number 12 bus.
10.	_____	He bought	a new record.
11.	_____	She saw	him in the street.
12.	_____	She stuck	them on the envelope.
13.	_____	She caught	it at the bus stop.
14.	_____	She got	on a train.
15.	_____	She put	it on the shelf.

E. What does Scott usually do?

What did he do yesterday?

1. _Scott gets up at 7:00._

   Scott got up at 7:00.

2. _____

   _____

3. _____

   _____

4. _____

   _____

5. _____

   _____

6. _____

   _____

7. _____

   _____

8. _____

   _____

F. Bill's father was born in London in 1925. He lived in London until 1930. Then his father sent him to a school in Yorkshire, where he lived until 1936. Then he went to a school in Sussex. In 1940 he became a soldier and was sent to North Africa to fight in the war. When he came back in 1944 he went to Oxford to study. In 1951 he became a doctor and began working outside London.

Answer the questions:

1. When did Bill's father live in London?   *He lived there from 1925 to 1930.*

2. When was he at school in Yorkshire?   _____

3. When was he at school in Sussex?   _____

4. When did he fight in the war?   _____

5. When did he study at Oxford?   _____

6. How long did he live in London?   *He lived there for five years.*

7. How long did he go to school in Yorkshire?   _____

8. How long did he go to school in Sussex?   _____

9. How long was he a soldier?   _____

10. How long did he study at Oxford?   _____

11. How long has he been a doctor now?   _____

G. Charlotte's mother has had many jobs.

1965	Secretary	1971	Assistant manager
1967	Department store clerk	1972	Boutique manager
1968	Night manager	1978	Boutique owner

Answer the questions:

1. When was Charlotte's mother a clerk?   *She was a clerk in 1967.*

2. How long was she a clerk?   _____

3. When did she begin her job as a night manager?   _____

4. When did she change jobs next?   _____

5. How long was she a boutique manager?   _____

. Presentation   Perfect tenses

The perfect tenses are used to express the completion of an action by a given time. They use a form of the verb *have* and a past participle.

Present perfect   Past perfect   Future perfect

I have read that book.   He had already left.   I shall have done it.
                           (by the time I arrived)   (by next week)

Perfect tenses are not used if we are interested in the specific time an action took place.

I read that book last week. (specific)
I have already read that book.
He left at one o'clock. (specific)
He had left before I arrived.

Present perfect

The present perfect tense is used with *since* and denotes a definite time in the past until now.

Donald has lived in Santa Clara since 1968. He has lived with us since his mother died.

The present perfect tense is used with *for* and denotes a period of time until now.

I have lived here for over ten years. My sister hasn't seen me for weeks.

Practice

A. Have you called Donald
   lately?   January   *I haven't called him since January.*

 1. Have you traveled
    lately?   March   _____

 2. Have you visited
    California recently?   July   _____

 3. Have you worked this
    year?   November   _____

 4. Have you talked to my
    brother recently?   last month   _____

B. Did you have a vacation
last month?   years   *I haven't had a vacation for years.* _____

   1. Did you travel to Santa
Clara last week?   months   _____

   2. Did you call Donald
this week?   weeks   _____

   3. Did you visit New York
recently?   years   _____

   4. Did you call my brother
last week?   months   _____

C. Why don't you write a letter?   *I have already written a letter.* _____

   1. Why don't you forgive your brother?   _____

   2. Why don't you go to see him?   _____

   3. Why don't you choose a gift for him?   _____

   4. Why don't you give him a call?   _____

D. Why don't you switch off the TV?   *I have already switched it off!* _____

   1. Why don't you close the window?   _____

   2. Why don't you move the table?   _____

   3. Why don't you return the money?   _____

   4. Why don't you answer the question?   _____

   5. Why don't you have your dinner?   _____

E. Fill in the blanks with *for* or *since*.

Donald has lived in Santa Clara ____ *since* ____ 1974. He has lived there _____

how many years? Yes, _____ ten years. Before he lived in Tucson _____

four years. _____ his arrival in Santa Clara he has been very fond of working in

the garden. He hasn't been back to Tucson _____ 1974. He has a very beautiful

garden with lovely roses. He hopes that he will be able to have the roses _____

many years to come. _____ how many years do you think he will have them?

F. What about you?

    1. How long have you spoken English?   *I have spoken English for* _____

    2. How long have you gone to school?   _____

    3. How long have you lived here?   _____

    4. How long have you worked?   _____

    5. How long have you known your best
       friend?   _____

G. Did they spend a lot of money?

   They have always spent a lot of money. _____

    1. Did they sell newspapers?

   _____

    2. Did they go to bed late?

   _____

    3. Did they ask for money?

   _____

    4. Did they drink milk?

   _____

    5. Did they tell lies?

   _____

    6. Did they take a vacation to Maine?

   _____

    7. Did they eat lobster and steak at Andrés?

   _____

    8. Did they visit their grandmother on Christmas?

   _____

14. Presentation   Past perfect

The past perfect tense describes a relationship between two different time situations. It uses a past form of *have* and a past participle.

Nigel *had moved* to Spain before you decided to go there. He *had read* about the weather before you told him about it.

The past perfect tense is also used in reported speech about something that happened in the simple past or present perfect tense.

Nigel said that he *had gotten* the idea years before. He said that his brother *had* finally *convinced* him to move.

Practice

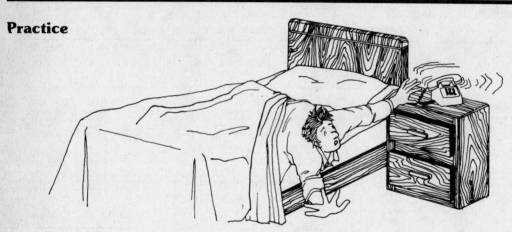

A. Follow the pattern.

1. Nigel fell out of bed and then the phone rang.
   Nigel had already fallen out of bed when the phone rang.

2. He sang a song and then he heard it on the radio.

   _____

3. Nigel went into the garden and then his mother came.

   _____

4. He wrote a letter and then the mail came.

   _____

5. He gave his mother a kiss and then she gave him one.

   _____

B. Nigel was standing at the train station. *He had just missed the train.*
   (miss the train)

   1. He was waiting for a taxi. _____
      (arrive)

   2. Nigel was looking at his money. _____
      (receive)

   3. I was sitting in my car. _____
      (get there)

   4. I was listening to the radio. _____
      (switch it on)

   5. Nigel was looking at the ground. _____
      (drop watch)

C. Follow this pattern.

   1. I saw Nigel.

      Yes, you told me you had seen Nigel yesterday.

   2. He never replied.

      _____

   3. He went to Spain.

      _____

   4. He did very well out there.

      _____

D. I hit the fence. *I had never hit the fence before.*

   1. I cut my arm. _____

   2. I quit my job. _____

   3. I hurt my leg. _____

   4. I read that book. _____

Check

A. Six years ago I met Nigel in Germany. We worked together in a factory from January to June. Then I went home to England again. Last March a friend of mine told me that he had met Nigel in London. Nigel had promised to telephone me as soon as he had time. But it was not until three weeks later that he found time. He telephoned on Thursday and said he would finish his job on Saturday and then come by train to London. I went to the station to meet him. The train should have arrived at two o'clock, but because of the snow and bad weather it didn't arrive until four o'clock.

1. How long had I known Nigel? _I had known Nigel for six years._

2. How long had we worked together? _____

3. How long had I waited for a telephone call? _____

4. How long had Nigel had to work? _____

5. How long had I waited at the station? _____

B. Five years ago Nigel met Angela. They dated for several months. Angela lived in Bonn. Nigel moved to a small apartment in Bonn and lived there from March to September. Later, Nigel received a big job promotion and moved to Italy. He lived there for three years. Angela missed Nigel so she moved there, too. I just heard that Nigel and Angela were married last month. Now they both live in Germany once again.

1. How long had Nigel known Angela? _He had known Angela for five years._

2. How long had they dated? _____

3. How long had Nigel lived in Bonn? _____

4. How long did they live in Italy? _____

5. How long had Nigel and Angela been married? _____

5. Presentation   Future perfect

Future perfect tense expresses something that will be completed in the future. It uses the verb phrase *will* + *have* + past participle. An indication about a future time is included in the statement to show by what time the action will be completed.

John *will have completed* his sociology exam by nine o'clock. He *will* already *have studied* hard for this test by the time he sits down to take it.

Practice

A. John is going to graduate from college in June. He is going to move to New Orleans in July. Then John is going to find an apartment. He is going to look for a job. He is going to make some new friends. John is going to save some money by the fall.

What will John have done by the fall?

1. *John will have graduated from college by the fall.*

2. _____

3. _____

4. _____

5. _____

6. _____

B. John is planning to go to graduate school in New York next year. He is going to begin to study law. John is going to adjust to life in New York. He is going to discover many wonderful places to see. John is going to learn about public transportation in the city. He is going to visit some old friends.

What will John have done by the end of next year?

1. *John will have gone to graduate school.*

2. _____

3. _____

4. _____

5. _____

6. _____

16. Presentation   Direct and indirect speech

Direct speech relates the speaker's precise words. We repeat the speaker's message by putting it in quotation marks and inserting a comma after the introductory verb. Verbs such as *say, reply, shout, cry, warn, direct, ask,* etc. are used to introduce the statement.

Stephen said, "I am happy." I replied, "I am so glad for you."

However, indirect speech does not repeat the speaker's words. Instead, only the meaning of the statement is relayed.

Stephen said he was happy. I replied I was glad for him.

Tenses change when speech is transformed from direct to indirect:

Direct	Indirect
Present	*Past*
Diane said, "I *love* him."	Diane said that she *loved* him.
He said, "She *is* a wonderful person."	He said that she *was* a wonderful person.
Tom asked, "*Is* she happy?"	Tom asked if she *was* happy.
Present Perfect	*Past Perfect*
He said, "I *have been* so lucky."	He said that he *had been* lucky.
We said, "We *have* often *thought* so too."	We said that we *had thought* so too.
We asked, "*Have* they *arrived*?"	We asked if they *had arrived*.
Will	*Would*
He asked, "*Will* you marry me?"	He asked if she *would* marry him.
She replied, "I *will* marry you."	She replied she *would* marry him.
She wondered, "*Will* they be late?"	She wondered if they *would* be late.

Practice

A. Rewrite these statements as indirect speech.

Mr. Perez says:

1. "I am tired."   *He said that he was tired.*

2. "I have to go home." _____

3. "I have a headache." _____

4. "I stop working at 5:00." _____

5. "I drive to the office." _____

B. Restate these in indirect speech.

1. I want a single room.   *I said that I wanted a single room.*

2. He wants to eat dinner. _____

3. He has to visit some clients. _____

4. Would you like to visit friends? _____

5. We have plans for tomorrow. _____

6. I have to stay in the city longer. _____

7. He wants to do more business. _____

8. He likes his job. _____

Check

Rewrite this conversation as indirect speech. Remember to use various verbs such as *reply*, *answer*, *exclaim*, *indicate* and *respond* among others to introduce the statements.

Mr. Perez: Are you interested in our newest product?

Client: I'm not sure.

Mr. Perez: Can I tell you a little bit about it?

Client: Of course.

Mr. Perez: This instrument measures and calculates the amount of electricity needed to operate your equipment at its fullest potential.

Client: It sounds useful.

Mr. Perez: Yes, and this instrument also tells you how to conserve energy and decrease costs.

Client: Wonderful!

Mr. Perez: However, this new product does cost close to a thousand dollars.
     Client: That's all right. I'm sure that we'll save money in the long run.
Mr. Perez: Then is it a sale?
     Client: You bet!

1. *Mr. Perez asked if the client was interested in the newest product.*

2. _____

3. _____

4. _____

5. _____

6. _____

7. _____

8. _____

9. _____

10. _____

11. _____

12. _____

7. Presentation   Tag questions

Tag questions are very short yes/no questions which are added to statements. They occur more often in conversation than they do in written statements. More often than not, the speaker is simply requesting verification of the statement.

The tag question is negative when the statement is affirmative. It is affirmative when the statement is negative. The second word of the tag question is generally the subject used in the sentence. The main verb of the tag question is usually some form of the verb *do*.

Alicia wants to go to the movies, *doesn't* she? She and her brother just came back from vacation, *didn't* they?

The exceptions to this rule are the modal verbs, the verb *to be*, and in British English, the verb *to have*.

We are going to the movies tonight, *aren't* we? You haven't seen the movie, *have* you? We should get there on time, *shouldn't* we? We can take the bus to the movies, *can't* we?

Practice

A. Use *are, aren't, have* or *don't* in these tag questions.

1. We are anxious to see this particular movie, ____*aren't*____ we?

2. The stars are wonderful actors, _____ they?

3. We haven't got much time, _____ we?

4. Your cousins aren't interested in going with us, _____ they?

5. The tickets aren't expensive, _____ they?

6. You have some money, _____ you?

7. Jack is meeting us here, _____ he?

8. We have got the best seats in the place, _____ we?

9. You haven't been to this theater before, _____ you?

10. We are having a wonderful time, _____ we?

11. I am enjoying myself, _____ I?

12. We are going to do it again sometime, _____ we?

B. Use *is*, *isn't*, *has* or *doesn't* in these tag questions.

1. That actress is beautiful, _____*isn't*_____ she?

2. She has nice hair, _____ she?

3. The director isn't very experienced, _____ he?

4. He hasn't ever directed a musical before, _____ he?

5. This theater is huge, _____ it?

6. It hasn't been open very long, _____ it?

7. The popcorn is delicious, _____ it?

8. This film isn't very old, _____ it?

9. Your sister isn't going with us, _____ she?

10. She hasn't gone out on a Saturday in weeks, _____ she?

11. She isn't interested in film, _____ she?

12. She is more interested in ballet, _____ she?

C. Use *do*, *don't*, *does*, *doesn't*, *did* or *didn't* in these tag questions.

1. Your sister likes modern dance too, _____*doesn't*_____ she?

2. Her favorite troupe performs at Metropolitan Center, _____ they?

3. She saw them dance last year, _____ she?

4. You don't care for dance, _____ you?

5. Your brother enjoys sports, _____ he?

6. You don't play tennis, _____ you?

7. Your brother won a tournament, _____ he?

8. They gave him a trophy, _____ they?

9. Your cousins also play well, _____ they?

10. Marilyn didn't win the tournament, _____ she?

11. She doesn't even practice, _____ she?

12. The judges didn't score fairly, _____ they?

13. I don't sound biased, _____ I?

14. You don't want to go to the game next week, _____ you?

15. We did have a good time, _____ we?

D. Use *can* or *can't* in these tag questions.

1. You can play tennis, ____*can't*____ you?

2. You can't play golf though, _____ you?

3. Your friends can't come to the party, _____ they?

4. They can drive, _____ they?

5. I can ask some others to come, _____ I?

6. My brother can come, _____ he?

7. I can make the salad, _____ I?

8. You can't come until nine o'clock, _____ you?

E. Use *could, couldn't, should, shouldn't, would* or *wouldn't* in these tag questions.

1. I probably shouldn't go out tonight, _____ I?

2. Marie could go to the party alone, _____ she?

3. Stan couldn't take her, _____ he?

4. I should call and cancel my reservation, _____ I?

5. You would like to go out to eat, _____ you?

6. I wouldn't drive there on that road, _____ you?

7. They couldn't find their way there, _____ they?

8. Hank shouldn't drive so fast, _____ he?

9. He could slow down, _____ he?

10. I wouldn't want to drive with him every day, _____ you?

18. Presentation   Progressive continuous

Progressive continuous is used to describe an action that is happening just now or during a particular time.

I *am painting* the house and my wife, Suzanne, *is working* on the car. The neighbors *are looking* at us. Yesterday I *was washing* the clothes and my wife *was mowing* the lawn. The neighbors *were staring* at us then too.

Progressive continuous is also used to show an action taking place when something else is happening.

I *was painting* the fence when the children came home. They *had been walking* home when it began to rain.

Progressive continuous also gives an indication that an action is expected, planned, or about to happen.

We *are going* to the party. My mother *is bringing* her delicious carrot cake. My wife *is planning* to show the slides of our vacation in British Columbia. We *are going* to have a good time.

Present continuous	*Past continuous*	*Future continuous*
I am	I was	I will be
He is + verb + *ing*	She was + verb + *ing*	She will be + verb + *ing*
They are	They were	You will be

Present perfect continuous

I *have been doing* many chores around the house lately. My wife *has been working* very hard also.

Past perfect continuous

We *had been thinking* of selling our house. My wife *had been talking* about moving to Canada.

Future continuous

We *will be seeing* our friends at a party tomorrow night. My parents *will be going* too.

Future perfect continuous

I *will have been sleeping* two hours by the time you get home.

Practice

A. What's Neal doing?   *Neal is painting the fence.*

1. What's Suzanne doing?   _____

2. What are the children doing?

_____

3. What are the dogs doing?

_____

4. What are the neighbors doing?

_____

B. What were they doing when you arrived?

They were watching TV.

1. What was Suzanne doing when they called?

2. What were his parents doing when he got there?

3. What was Suzanne doing when Neal was eating?

4. What were the neighbors doing when Neal and Suzanne came home?

C. Complete the dialogues.

—Where have you been all this time?

—I've been cutting the grass.

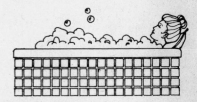

1. Where has Suzanne been all this time?

— _____

2. Where have the children been?

— _____

3. Where has Neal been all this time?

— _____

4. Where has Suzanne been all this time?

— _____

D. All of these people are going on vacation. What will they be doing?

1. Neal

Neal will be skiing.

2. Mother and
   Suzanne

_____

3. Suzanne

_____

4. Arthur

_____

E. When are you leaving on
   your trip?   twelfth   *I'm leaving on the twelfth.*

   1. When is Joan coming?   Monday   _____

   2. When are you going?   tomorrow   _____

   3. When is the plane leaving? 7:15   _____

   4. When is his train
      arriving?   noon   _____

F. Why aren't you working?   ill   *I should have been working but I'm ill.*

   1.   painting the house?   tired   _____

   2.   helping your wife?   lazy   _____

   3. Why aren't you playing
       golf?   late   _____

   4.   watching TV?   busy   _____

G. Haven't they arrived yet?   *They should be arriving any minute now.*

   1. Hasn't the plane landed yet?   _____

   2. Haven't they gone yet?   _____

   3. Haven't they come yet?   _____

   4. Hasn't the train left yet?   _____

Check

Fill in the blanks with the progressive continuous form of the verb.

1. Suzanne _has been dreaming_ about moving to Canada for years. (dream)

2. She _____ there when she first met Neal. (live)

3. They _____ to college then. (go)

4. Neal's parents _____ to New York this year. (move)

5. His father _____ a business there. (start)

6. Neal _____ the house just in case they do move. (paint)

7. Meanwhile, Maurice and Joan _____ their vacation. (plan)

8. They _____ on a camping trip to Canada. (go)

9. They _____ about it even before Neal and Suzanne mentioned their plans. (think)

10. They _____ what to do when they return from their vacation. (decide)

19. Presentation   Present participle — -ing form

Some verbs use the -ing form as their object, but never take an infinitive.

admit	deny	go on	recall	suggest
appreciate	enjoy	keep	regret	understand
avoid	finish	keep on	risk	doesn't mind
can't help	get through	postpone	spend	sit
consider	give up	practice	stop*	

Max *admitted watching* Irene at the nightclub. She was the best dancer there. Now, he *regretted telling* her that he was a good dancer. Max *avoided asking* Irene to dances. He *kept losing* his courage. Finally, Irene *suggested going* to a dance. Max *admitted not knowing* how to dance. But, Irene *didn't mind teaching* him how. Max really *enjoyed being* with Irene.

*Stop can take an infinitive at times; however, it is a modifier which only expresses purpose.

Max stopped to look at the other dancers. (in order to)

Some verbs can be followed by an -ing form or an infinitive.

attempt	intend	plan	try
begin	like	prefer	
continue	neglect	start	

-ing form	to + infinitive
Max attempted dancing a waltz.	Max attempted to dance a waltz.
Max preferred going to the movies.	Max preferred to go to the movies.
He liked skiing with Irene too.	Max liked to ski with Irene too.

The -ing form can be used immediately after *before, after, until, since, when* and *while* when verbs have the same subject.

Max left for the dance *before finishing* his work. (before he finished . . .)
Irene was always quiet *when listening* to the music. (when she listened . . .)

The -ing form is also used after prepositions.

Max thanked Irene *for teaching* him how to dance. He is looking *forward to going* to the next dance.

Verbs having to do with the senses (seeing, hearing, feeling, touching, etc.) may use the -ing form or the infinitive.

Max watched her dance/dancing. He heard her whisper/whispering and noticed her smile/smiling.

Practice

A. Is Irene still dancing? saw *I saw her dancing.* _____

  1. Is Max still singing? heard _____

  2. Are the musicians still
    playing? listened _____

  3. Is Max still working? watched _____

  4. Is Irene still skiing? saw _____

B. Max washed my car. *I hope you paid him for washing it.* _____

  1. Suzanne cut my lawn. _____

  2. The children cleaned
    my room. _____

  3. Neal painted my fence. _____

  4. Suzanne fixed my car. _____

C. Max doesn't want to make mistakes.   *He's afraid of making mistakes.*

   1. Irene doesn't want to show her feelings.   _____

   2. Max doesn't want to get married.   _____

   3. They don't want to get laughed at.   _____

   4. We don't want to forget the secret.   _____

D. Max worked the whole winter.   *He spent the whole winter working.*

   1. He delivered groceries every morning.   _____

   2. Irene danced at the nightclub every
       night.   _____

   3. They played tennis on most weekends.   _____

   4. Max listens to the radio most of the day.   _____

   5. He watched Irene every minute.   _____

E. How would you respond to these statements?

   1. My hair is long.   *Yes, it needs cutting, doesn't it?*

   2. My pencil is very dull.   _____

   3. My shirt is dirty.   _____

   4. The lawn has many weeds.   _____

   5. Someone should speak to him.   _____

F. Follow this pattern.

Max is interested in reading books but isn't very fond of playing the piano.

1. _____

2. _____

3. _____

4. _____

5. _____

G. Why can't you speak English?   *I'm not used to speaking English.* _____

   1.   knit your own sweaters?   _____

   2.   wash the dishes?   _____

   3. Why can't you do your own homework? _____

   4.   sew your own clothes?   _____

   5.   fix the car?   _____

H. Do you like to go to restaurants?   *I'm tired of going to restaurants.* _____

   1.   listen to records?   _____

   2.   have an early breakfast?   _____

   3. Do you like to do exercises?   _____

   4.   go to bed late?   _____

   5.   wait for your best friend?   _____

I . I wanted to help the old lady, but he stopped me.
He stopped me from helping the old lady. _____

   1. I wanted to swim across the river, but he stopped me.

   _____

   2. She wanted to give up her job, but he stopped her.

   _____

   3. They wanted to drive the car, but he stopped them.

   _____

   4. We wanted to borrow money from the bank, but he stopped us.

   _____

   5. We wanted to go for a walk, but he stopped us.

   _____

Check

A. 1. Suzanne is used to _____*working*_____ late. (work)

2. She is very interested in _____ to Canada. (move)

3. She can't help _____ so much. (dream)

4. Neal enjoys _____ with his children. (play)

5. I thought I saw him _____ a while ago. (eat)

6. Neal is always _____ the clothes for the family. (wash)

7. Max is fond of _____. (dance)

8. Irene likes _____ him how to dance. (teach)

9. Max also enjoys _____ with Irene. (ski)

10. He loves _____ with her all the time. (be)

B. Write some things that you are tired of:

1. doing every day   *I'm tired of* _____

2. having for lunch   _____

3. hearing   _____

4. seeing   _____

5. listening to   _____

20. Presentation . **Auxiliary verb and the simple form**

The words *must, may, can, let, should, will, shall, do not* and *does not* are signal words (or auxiliary verbs) that can be used before the simple form.

I *must go* to the theater right away. I *shall walk* there. You *can come* too. Meryl *may help* us with the show. Andrea *will do* a great deal of work, too. The boys in the cast *do not work* very hard. Russ *doesn't work* at all! He *let* Meryl *drive* to rehearsal. He *may* not *come* today.

When making a statement about something that needs to be done or accomplished, the signal words *had better* are used directly before the simple form.

We *had better walk* fast or we will be late for the rehearsal. Andrea *had better bring* her sewing machine or we will not get all the costumes sewn. Russ *had better come* to more rehearsals or he won't know his part in the play.

Practice

A. Who drove, you or Meryl?

> *I let Meryl drive.*
>
> *Meryl let me drive.*

1. Who paid for the show, you or Russ?

2. Who asked for the money, you or Meryl?

3. Who helped with the show, you or Andrea?

4. Who sewed the costumes, you or Meryl?

B. Write answers using *had better*.

1. It's cold. *I had better wear a coat.*

2. It's late. *We*

3. It's raining. *Meryl*

4. It's windy. *Andrea*

1. Presentation   Verb + object + infinitive

Several verbs need an object plus *to* and an infinitive to complete the statement.

advised	commanded	forced	obliged	teach	wanted
asked	convinced	get	ordered	tell	would like
allowed	encouraged	hired	permit	told	
begged	expected	instructed	persuaded	urged	
caused	forbid	invited	requested	waited for	

Liz is a career counselor. She *encouraged* clients to search for good careers. Liz *advised* Joshua to get a job in the electronics industry. She *convinced* him to go back to college. Liz *persuaded* him to register for classes in the spring. She *wanted* Joshua to get a good job.

Practice

A. Fill in the appropriate form of the verbs to complete the sentences.

ask	want	expect	told	urge
convince	hire	remind	force	persuade

1. Liz ____wanted____ Joshua to get a job.

2. She _____ him to register for classes.

3. She _____ him to go to the college the next day.

4. Liz _____ Joshua to sign up for several classes.

5. Liz knew that electronics firms _____ students.

6. She _____ Joshua to get good grades in school.

7. Joshua _____ Liz to write a letter of recommendation for him.

8. He _____ himself to study hard.

9. Joshua _____ friends to go visit Liz.

10. He _____ them to look for good jobs too.

B. What did Joshua's mother want him to do?

1.   *She wanted him to go to school.*

2.   _____

3.   _____

4.   _____

5.   _____

6.   _____

C. Fill in the appropriate form of the verbs to complete the sentences.

permit	ask	beg	cause
encourage	want	advise	expect

1. Joshua's friend, Nancy, __*asked*__ Liz to help her.
2. Liz _____ her to pursue a career in teaching.
3. Liz's advice _____ Nancy to think about teaching.
4. She _____ her parents to allow her to return to school.
5. They _____ her to register for classes.
6. However, they _____ Nancy to work on weekends.
7. They _____ her to pay for her own tuition.
8. Nancy's parents _____ her to learn the true value of education.

22. Presentation   Verb + infinitive

Some verbs are followed by the infinitive in order to complete a statement.

agree	consent	fail	intend	offer	refuse
attempt	continue	forgot	learn	plan	remember
begin	decide	hesitate	mean	prefer	start
care	desire	hope	neglect	promise	try
					want

Grace *decided* to travel to San Francisco. She *intended* to drive by herself. She *planned* to visit friends along the way. She *refused* to worry about the journey. In fact, she *preferred* to go alone.

Practice

A. Grace drove to California.   *She decided to drive to California.*

1. She bought a new car.   _____

2. Grace called her friends.   _____

3. She told them that she was going to visit.   _____

4. Grace learned how to fix her car.   _____

5. She planned to stay for a month.   _____

B. Fill in the appropriate form of the verb to complete the sentences.

continue	start	intend	hope
promise	try	refuse	prefer

1. Grace __*preferred*__ to drive during the day.

2. She _____ to plan her trip in August.

3. Grace _____ to see a lot of the country.

4. She _____ to study the maps until she was ready to leave.

5. Grace _____ to believe that she would get lost on the way.

6. She _____ to make it to California in five days.

7. She _____ to drive ten hours a day.

8. She _____ to send postcards to all of her friends.

23. Presentation   Passive and active voice

The active voice form of the verb describes what the subject does.

My dog chases cats. Even the smallest cat frightens my dog.

The passive voice form of the verb describes what is done to the subject.

Cats are chased by my dog. My dog is frightened by even the smallest cat.

Practice

A. Answer in the passive voice.

1. Why does your dog chase my cat?

   Cats are always chased by dogs.

2. Why do you plant your trees in spring?

   _____

3. Why do you send your letters by air mail?

   _____

4. Why does the mail carrier deliver your package?

   _____

5. Why do secretaries type your letters?

   _____

6. Why does the customs agent search the passengers?

   _____

B. Have they told you who won?

   I'll be told who won later.

1. Have they taught you how to play basketball?

   _____

2. Have they asked you to join the club?

   _____

3. Have they paid you for your work?

   _____

4. Have they given you your report card?

   _____

5. Have they told you about your new roommate?

   _____

C. Follow the pattern.

   1. First we harvest the wheat, then we take it to the flour mills.
     When the wheat has been harvested, it's taken to the flour mills.

   2. First we grind the corn into flour, then we sell it to the bakers.

     _____

   3. First we mix the flour with milk, then we make it into bread.

     _____

   4. First we peel the potatoes, then we boil them.

     _____

   5. First we pick the apples, then we sell them.

     _____

   6. First we slice the bread, then we butter it.

     _____

D. When must we mail the letter?   *It must be mailed at once.*

   1. When must we pay the bill?   _____

   2. When must we send the package?   _____

   3. When must we make the bed?   _____

   4. When must we clean the window?   _____

E. When will they mail the letter?   *It will be mailed this afternoon.*

   1. When will they send the package?   _____

   2. When will they write the telegram?   _____

   3. When will they mend the bike?   _____

   4. When will they paint the garage?   _____

   5. When will they sort the mail?   _____

4. Presentation   Auxiliary verbs—modals

The auxiliary verbs (or modals) occur only in the simple present and past tenses. These verbs: *can/could, shall/should-ought, will/would, may/might* and *must* are always followed by the infinitive form of the verb. These modals indicate ability, permission, obligation, possibility, etc. and do not take regular verb endings.

John *can* write his own songs. (ability)
He *could* play guitar when he was thirteen years old. (past ability)
Shall I ask him to come to our party? (advisability)
We *should* ask all of his other friends to come too. (obligation)
He *ought* to be surprised! (expectation)
John *will* entertain us all with his music. (promise)
He *would* have arrived sooner if he had known we were having such a big party. (contrary to fact)
We *may* ask him to sing our favorite song. (permission)
He *might* play his latest song. (conjecture)
You *must* hear that one! (necessity)

Modal verbs do *not* use do-does-did in questions and negative statements.

Can you play guitar? *Would* you like to learn to play? *Will* you be coming to the party? I *could* not possibly come to the party. I *will* not have the time.

25. Presentation   Can/could/be able to

The modal verbs *can* and *could* take these forms in the present and past tenses.

Present	Past
can	could
cannot	could not
can't	couldn't
Can I?	Could I?
Can't I?	Couldn't I?

I can sing. I can dance. I could sing when I was two years old and I could dance when I was three.

An alternative form of the modals *can* and *could* is *be able to*.

	I	am
Present	They	are
	S(he)	is
Past	They	were
	S(he)	was

able to sing and dance.

	We	have been
Present/	They	had been
Past	S(he)	has been
Perfect		
Future	They	will be
	I	shall be

Practice

A. Can you help me now?

No, I can't but I'll be able to help you soon.

1. Can he drive now?

_____

2. Can she find a job now?

_____

3. Can they give me the money now?

_____

4. Can you borrow this record now?

_____

B. What about you? Write five things you *couldn't* do ten years ago but that you can do now.

Example: _Ten years ago I couldn't read, but now I can._

1. _____

2. _____

3. _____

4. _____

5. _____

C. Now write five things you *can't* do now but that you hope you will be able to do in five years.

Example: _I can't drive a car now, but I'll be able to in five years._

1. _____

2. _____

3. _____

4. _____

5. _____

D. Fill in the blanks with *can, could* or *will be able to*.

1. I hope I _____can_____ see you next month.

2. He said that he _____ come.

3. I _____ never remember the word. It is always like that.

4. I _____ not say I'm happy here.

5. When _____ you _____ buy that house?

6. I _____ understand what he said.

7. I hope I _____ get there in time.

8. This morning Jose _____ not find his English textbook.

9. Next year Aki _____ get his driver's license.

10. Last night _____ not fall asleep.

11. Yesterday Betsy _____ answer all the teacher's questions.

12. I hope I _____ work harder next year.

E. Did Juanita catch the bus?   go earlier

No, but she could have caught the bus if she had gone earlier.
_____

1. Did they get good seats at the basketball game?   pay more

_____

2. Did you buy a car?   have enough money

_____

3. Did you see the parade?   wait two hours

_____

4. Did she leave at seven o'clock?   get up in time

_____

5. Did they go to bed late?   ask their parents

_____

6. Did he win the race?   run faster

_____

7. Did you speak English?   be in America

_____

8. Did they learn Spanish?   teach it

_____

6. Presentation   May/might

The past form of the verb *may* is *might*.
An alternative form of this modal is *be allowed to/be permitted to*.

I	am
They	are
S(he)	is
They	were
S(he	was

allowed to go to the beach.

We	have been
S(he)	has been
They	will be
I	shall be

The modals *may* or *might* are used to express possibility.

It *may* be true. It *might* be true.
She *may* have missed the train home. She *might* have missed the train home.

Practice

A. Why must we hurry? Are we late?

If we don't hurry we may be late.

1. Why must we find a gas station? Are we running out of gas?

_____

2. Why must we leave early? Will we miss the show?

_____

3. Why must we work harder? Will we lose our jobs?

_____

4. Why must we go now? Will we miss the bus?

_____

5. Why must we study every night? Will we fail our tests?

_____

B. May we park here?   *We were allowed to park here yesterday.*

   1. May she go home early?   _____

   2. May they come?   _____

   3. May we use this typewriter?   _____

   4. May I do that?   _____

   5. May he walk to the store with you?   _____

C. Did Julie take the bus?   train
She might have taken the train instead.

   1. Did Bill leave at eight o'clock?   nine

   _____

   2. Did his mother go to Kansas?   Arizona

   _____

   3. Did Bill buy a new car?   bike

   _____

   4. Did your friends order champagne?   soft drinks

   _____

   5. Did they sell their house?   boat

   _____

D. I was surprised they entered the country.   *They were allowed to enter the country.*

   1.   she took pictures.   _____

   2.   they bought the diamonds.   _____

   3. I was surprised he visited the prison.   _____

   4.   they built on this site.   _____

7. Presentation Must

Present	Past
must	must is used only in indirect speech

An alternative form of the modal *must* is *to have to.*

Present	I We S(he)	have to have to has to
Past	S(he) We	had to had to
Perfect	S(he) We	has had to have had to . . . .
Past Perfect	S(he) We	had had to had had to
Future	I We	will have to will have to

Other alternative forms that say the same thing are: *to be obliged to, to be compelled to* and *to be forced to.*

I have to go to my parents' for dinner.	= I am obliged to go to my parents' for dinner.
I have to get good grades on my exam.	= I am compelled to get good grades on my exams.
I have to stay in bed.	= I am forced to stay in bed.

Practice

A. Did you have to pay the bills today?   next week

No, I didn't. I must pay them next week.
_____

1. Did you have to go to the dentist this week?   on Monday

_____

2. Did you have to fix the car?   later

_____

3. Did you have to turn off the TV at nine?   ten o'clock

_____

4. Did you have to buy a new car?   soon

_____

B. Now write the same sentences but use *have to* instead.

No, I didn't. I'll have to pay them next week. _____

1. _____
2. _____
3. _____
4. _____

C. Does your husband always have
   to work hard?   *No, but he had to work hard yesterday.*

   1.   wash up?   _____

   2.   go to bed early?   _____

   3. Does your husband always have
      to get up at 6?   _____

   4.   make the bed?   _____

   5.   help with the housework? _____

D. Write these sentences in the past tense.

   1. I must say goodbye.   *I had to say goodbye.* _____

   2. I must work as hard as I can. _____

   3. She has to wash the dishes.   _____

   4. He has to vacuum the rug.   _____

   5. We have to begin before five o'clock. _____

   6. We must be home before dark.   _____

   7. They have to keep everything clean. _____

   8. She has to go home early.   _____

8. Presentation   **Shall/will**
Should/would/ought

The modals *shall* and *will* express future time.

I *shall* be forty on my next birthday. My husband *will* be forty on his next birthday, too. We *will* celebrate our birthdays by going out for dinner. I *shall* have the most expensive meal on the menu!

The modals *should* and *would* express a future in the past.

He said he *would* do it later. I said I *should* do it later too.

1. In many parts of the English speaking world, however, (especially in America) *will* is used in place of *shall* with the first person pronoun.

2. In spoken English, *I'll, you'll, he'll*, etc. stand for I will, you will, he will, etc.

3. In spoken English, *won't* stands for will not and *shan't* for shall not.

Should expresses obligations that are to be met, expectations or fulfillments of things that will probably happen and to offer advice.

Athletes *should* all be on strict diets. My friend, David, *should* compete in the race since he is physically fit. He *should* win all of the awards because he is such a fast runner.

Practice

A. My sister is twenty. How old will she be next year?

She will be twenty-one next year.

1. My brother is twelve. How old will he be in three years?

_____

2. My mother is forty-one. How old will she be in ten years?

_____

3. My father is thirty-nine. How old will he be on his next birthday?

_____

4. My grandmother is seventy-two. How old will she be in two years?

_____

B. Fill in the blanks with *will be* or *was*.

1. Tom is twenty-nine. He ____*will be*____ thirty next year.

2. Inez is fourteen. She _____ thirteen last year.

3. My uncle is sixty-eight. He _____ sixty-nine in April.

4. My aunt is fifty-seven. She _____ fifty-eight next week.

5. My cousin is thirty. She _____ twenty-six when she got married.

6. I _____ eighteen next week.

7. I _____ seventeen when I graduated.

8. Jim _____ forty-six when I first met him.

C. Respond to these statements any way you want.

1. Teddy has forgotten his wallet.
   Then he won't be able to spend any money, will he?

2. Teddy has left his camera at home.
   _____

3. Teddy can't find his glasses.
   _____

4. Teddy has broken his fishing rod.
   _____

D. I shall go.   *I said I should go.*

1. We shall win.   _____

2. They will be late.   _____

3. She will come later.   _____

4. You will help me.   _____

5. I shall never give up.   _____

E. Did you take the bus to the race?   taxi   _You should have taken the taxi._

  1. Did you get off at the cinema?   museum   _____

  2. Did you ask for directions to the stadium?   school   _____

  3. Did you go with Mr. Williams?   Mrs. Huang   _____

  4. Did you buy a ticket?   two tickets   _____

  5. Did you call Doug?   his sister   _____

  6. Did you listen to the radio?   read the newspaper   _____

F. Were you surprised when David won the race?   _No, I knew he would win._

  1. Were the others disappointed when they lost?   _____

  2. Was David surprised after he won the race?   _____

  3. Was he angry because Bill didn't come?   _____

  4. Was Bill disappointed when Lucy moved away?   _____

  5. Was David sad when you left?   _____

29. Presentation   Used to

Used to can serve as a way to describe something that is not applicable any more. Alternative forms of this phrase are *usually/generally* + verb or *be in the habit of* + verb + *ing*.

Myra *used to* get up quite early in the morning.
Myra generally got up at five o'clock.   (formerly but no longer)
Myra was in the habit of getting up at five.

An infinitive need not be repeated after *used to*. However *to be* may not be omitted.

Myra is not as young as she *used to be*. She does not work as hard as she *used to*.

Be used to plus *-ing* form is an idiom or common phrase that is utilized when talking about becoming or being accustomed to someone or something.

Suzanne is *used to* working hard. I am *used to* seeing her when she is incredibly busy.

Use can also serve as a regular verb.

Suzanne *used* her teaching background to help her develop confidence.
Myra *uses* her work as a means to socialize and meet new friends.

Practice

A. Was Myra upset about the bad weather?   *She is used to bad weather.*

1. Is he disappointed about the poor results?   _____

2. Were the customers angry about the prices?   _____

3. Was the baby disturbed by the noise?   _____

4. Was Suzanne upset about the work?   _____

5. Was she surprised by the negative response?   _____

B. What do you use to lock a door?   <u>*You use a key.*</u>

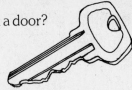

1. What did they use to get up
    on the roof?   _____

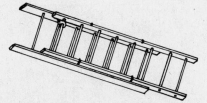

2. What did he use to cut the
    bread?   _____

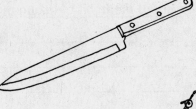

3. What did she use to cut the
    grass?   _____

4. What does he use to wash
    the car?   _____

5. What did they use to paint
the house?

_____

6. What did she use to brush
her teeth?

_____

C. Rewrite these sentences.

1. I usually take the bus.   *I am in the habit of taking the bus.*

2. He usually arrives at six o'clock.   _____

3. They generally get up at seven.   _____

4. I usually work until five.   _____

5. We generally went by car.   _____

D. Rewrite these sentences.

1. I was in the habit of going to bed early.   *I used to go to bed early.*

2. She was in the habit of taking a shower.   _____

3. We are in the habit of phoning each
other.   _____

4. I was in the habit of visiting her each
day.   _____

5. They were in the habit of going
out every night.   _____

0. Presentation   Be going to

The phrase *be going to* indicates that something will be taking place in the future. It signifies that an action is planned or imminent.

The Ortegas are going to take a vacation. (planned)
They were going to get away from it all. (intended)
The plane is going to leave at three o'clock. (imminent)
I think that they are going to have a good time. (probable)

Practice

A. Has Mr. Ortega already
   left?   soon   *He's going to leave soon.* _____

   1. Has Ralph already
      gotten up?   any minute   _____

   2. Has Mrs. Ortega
      already packed her
      suitcase?   this morning   _____

   3. Has Marlena already
      driven off?   within the hour   _____

   4. Has Mr. Ortega
      already gone to the
      airport?   at noon   _____

B. Have they already started?   *They're going to start soon.* _____

   1. Have they already taken a shower?   _____

   2. Have they already received their
      tickets?   _____

   3. Have they already packed their bags?   _____

   4. Have they already paid for their trip?   _____

C. Has it started raining?   *It's going to start raining soon.*

1. Has it stopped snowing?   _____

2. Has the sun set?   _____

3. Has it gotten dark outside?   _____

4. Has it gotten sunny yet?   _____

D. He used to be interested in writing.
   He was going to be a writer.

1. painting/painter

   _____

2. singing/singer

   _____

3. acting/actor

   _____

4. nursing/nurse

   _____

5. sailing/sailor

   _____

6. dancing/dancer

   _____

7. farming/farmer

   _____

8. typing/typist

   _____

9. flying/pilot

   _____

Part VIII/Prepositions

Alphabetic list of prepositions:

About
Above
According to
Across
After
Against
Along
Among
Around
As to, as for, etc.
At
Before
Behind
Below
Beneath
Beside
Besides
Between
Beyond
By
During
Except, save
For
For . . . sake
From

In
Into
Of
Off
On
Out of
Outside
Over
Owing to, because of, etc.
Past
Round, around
Since
Through
Till, until
To
Toward, towards
Under
With
Within
Without

Translate these sentences into your *own* language.

About

They spoke about you.

Tell me all about it.

What did you think about (of)?

I don't care about her.

Translation:

_____

_____

_____

_____

Above

The airplane flew above the clouds.

The water came above our knees.

The temperature has been above the average.

_____

_____

_____

According to

According to him, you are right.

You must play according to the rules.

According to the radio, the match was
  cancelled.

_____

_____

_____

Across

Eduardo swam across the river.

Will you help me across the street?

He stood with his arms folded across his chest.

I came across an old friend yesterday.

_____

_____

_____

_____

After

I'll see you after breakfast.

They were not back until after dark.

I'll start the day after tomorrow.

After that he never did it again.

The police are after you.

Shut the door after you.

My sister looked after our dog.

_____

_____

_____

_____

_____

_____

_____

Translation:

He takes after his father.

After all, we are in the same boat.

Against

The woman leaned against the tree.

She swam against the current.

He was against my idea.

She did it against her will.

Ago

The train left a few minutes ago.

It happened a long time ago.

How long ago is it since you last smoked?

Along

There are trees all along the river banks.

They walked along the street.

Note: adverbial use:

I said so all along.

Move along, please.

I get along well with her.

Among

She was sitting among her children.

Among other things, I don't like your tie!

It's wonderful to be among friends again.

He saw a man hiding among the bushes.

As to, as for, etc.

As for you, I hope never to see you again.

As to the price, we must talk about that later.

At

His brother lives at 90 Long Road.

Donna is staying at our house.

England was at war with Germany.

We were at work.

She never felt at ease in his house.

I'll do it at the first opportunity.

At Christmas. At Easter. At Midsummer.

At once.

At dawn. At dusk. At the end of May.

The boys threw stones at the dog.

The man shouted at me.

What are you driving at?

At any rate.

Do it at all costs.

The train arrived at Oxford at nine o'clock.

He was angry at being kept waiting.

Greg is very good (bad) at English.

I saw him at a distance.

Before

The man was brought before the judge.

She arrived before him.

Your name comes before mine in the alphabet.

I met him the day before yesterday.

It was just before one o'clock.

Translation:

_____

_____

_____

_____

_____

_____

_____

_____

_____

_____

_____

_____

_____

_____

_____

_____

_____

_____

_____

_____

_____

_____

_____

Behind

Shut the door behind you.

What is behind his decision?

He left nothing behind him when he died.

They landed five minutes behind time.

Below

The sun sinks below the horizon.

It is ten degrees below zero.

Some parts of Holland are below sea level.

Beneath

The water flows beneath the bridge.

It is beneath your dignity.

Their behavior is beneath contempt.

Beside

Who is sitting beside him?

Come and sit beside me.

She was beside herself with sorrow.

Besides

I have three other houses besides this one.

There were five of them besides the leader.

Between

The road runs between Concord and
Lexington.

They shared the food between them.

I saw a fight between a man and a woman.

Between you and me, this is crazy!

Translation:

_____

_____

_____

_____

_____

_____

_____

_____

_____

_____

_____

_____

_____

_____

_____

_____

_____

_____

Beyond

The town is beyond that hill.

I live beyond my income.

By

The cat was sitting by the window.

Our house is by the lake.

By the way, can you tell me what to say?

We went there by train but came back by air.

I sent the letter by air mail.

(In passive sentences:)

He was called Ted by everybody.

The dog was run over by a train.

I read a book by Harold Robbins.

She earns her living by teaching.

These cups are made by hand.

He is lazy by nature.

I know her by sight.

They did it little by little.

They entered two by two.

By my watch it is 2 o'clock.

Do you prefer travelling by night or by day?

They ought to be here by this time.

Don't you know better by now?

During

We never met during our childhood.

The student slept during the lecture.

It rained every day during our stay in France.

Translation:

_____

_____

_____

_____

_____

_____

_____

_____

_____

_____

_____

_____

_____

_____

_____

_____

_____

_____

_____

Except

We go to school every day except Sundays.

Nobody was there except me.

I looked everywhere except under the chair.

She did nothing except work.

I like your new hat except for the color.

For

He bought a book for me.

This gift is meant (intended) for someone else.

I need a stamp for this letter.

I had chicken for dinner.

Some people have coffee for breakfast.

They have gone for a walk.

What are you looking for?

You must send for a doctor at once.

Jogging is good for you.

He will be fit for work on Monday.

The soldier won a medal for bravery.

She could not speak for laughing.

The woman was punished for stealing.

I sold the car for a good price.

They drove for 60 miles.

Translate word for word.

For . . . sake

She did it for her brother's sake.

She did it for the sake of her health.

For old times sake.

Translation:

From

We went from New York to Los Angeles.

Where does he come from?

Can you see it from here?

Count from one to ten.

I borrowed the money from the bank.

What else can you expect from her?

I heard it from a friend of mine.

Where did you get this book from?

The old man suffered from rheumatism.

I am speaking from experience.

He tried to keep the news from me.

Here we are safe from any danger.

In

Mt. Everest is the highest mountain in the world.

What would you have done in my place?

He lives in the country.

He was sitting in an armchair.

I read about it in the newspaper.

He put his hand in (into) his pocket.

Cut the cake in two.

He went out in the rain.

They fell in love.

In the spring.

In /the year/ 1969. In the 18th century.

In January. In the 1960s.

Translation:

_____

_____

_____

_____

_____

_____

_____

_____

_____

_____

_____

_____

_____

_____

_____

_____

_____

_____

_____

_____

_____

Translation:

In the morning (afternoon, evening). _____

In the Middle Ages. _____

I'm going to America in a week. _____

I'll be ready in a moment. _____

I shall be back in a short time. _____

Can you finish the work in an hour? _____

A soldier in uniform. _____

They sat in the sun. _____

Sit in the shade. _____

She lost her way in the dark. _____

In despair he asked for help. _____

The girl was in tears. _____

Are you in a hurry? _____

Do it in secret. (In fun). _____

Do it in this manner. _____

What is that in English? _____

I believe in God. _____

At last I succeeded in passing the test. _____

Are you interested in history? _____

I have no confidence in you. _____

Into

We jumped into the water. _____

They got into trouble. _____

He got into difficulties. _____

The young girl burst into tears. _____

Translate the text into French. _____

They sat talking far into the night. _____

Of

The house is built of wood (stone, brick).

He died of cancer.

What were they thinking of (about)?

He spoke to me of (about) his job.

What are they talking of (about)?

I am not sure of (about) that.

Don't complain of a sore throat.

It was good (kind, nice) of your brother
  to come.

The witness was accused of lying.

They found him innocent of the crime.

It's characteristic of him.

This is very typical of her.

The basket was full of eggs.

Off

She fell off the roof.

Don't switch off the radio (the TV).

A button has come off my jacket.

He will be off duty soon.

Take your hands off my bag!

Keep off the grass.

On

There was a carpet on the floor.

Pictures were hanging on the walls.

I ate on the plane.

He lived on $15 a day.

What's on the radio tonight?

Translation:

_____

_____

_____

_____

_____

_____

_____

_____

_____

_____

_____

_____

_____

_____

_____

_____

_____

_____

_____

Translation:

I saw the match on TV.

We are not on the telephone.

London is on the Thames.

The house is on the shore.

On my return I shall help you.

I didn't meet him on that occasion.

I'm coming on Sunday.

She wrote a book on birds.

My father is away on business.

I am on duty from twelve to eight.

He is always on the go.

He is on his way to Rome.

You can depend on me.

On the whole, it's a good idea.

I didn't do it on purpose.

Have pity on me.

Cigarettes are on sale here.

The house is on fire.

On the contrary, I *do* like it.

Out of

She jumped out of bed.

She walked out of the shop.

I did it out of friendship.

They fled out of fear.

She asked out of curiosity.

I was quite out of money.

He is out of work.

I was out of breath.

I ran out of gas on the highway.

It is out of reach.

The plane is out of sight.

Over

We climbed over the wall.

There was no bridge over (across) the river.

I fell over a stone.

She spoke to me over her shoulder.

Who is the man over there?

He is just getting over his illness.

I'll be glad to show you over the school.

The President spoke for over (more than) an hour.

We had a nice talk over a couple of beers.

I still have not gotten over his death.

Owing to

We were late owing to the traffic.

The store was empty owing to the high prices.

Past

It is ten past six.

We went past the church.

He hurried past me without saying hello.

I had some difficulty in getting past the sentry.

These shoes are past mending.

Translation:

_____

_____

_____

_____

_____

_____

_____

_____

_____

_____

_____

_____

_____

_____

_____

_____

_____

_____

_____

Round, around

The earth moves round (AE around)* the sun.

He went round (AE around) the corner.

They were sitting round (AE around) the table.

The visitor looked round (AE around) the house.

Shall I show you round (AE around) the house?

(AE = American English)

Since

He has lived in Peru since 1980.

I have not seen him since last Monday.

He had been working since 10 o'clock.

They had not met since their schooldays.

Through

The road goes through the forest.

Mother came in through the window.

Go through these papers carefully.

An idea flashed through my mind.

It happened through no fault of hers.

Till (until)

I shall wait till (until) ten o'clock.

My mother works from morning till night.

Until now I knew nothing about you.

I am not free till one o'clock.

To

[With indirect object (dative object)]

I gave a doll to the little boy.

Translation:

_____

_____

_____

_____

_____

_____

_____

_____

_____

_____

_____

_____

_____

_____

_____

_____

_____

I gave the little boy a doll.

He lent his book to Mike.

Did you send that letter to him?

These examples show that the indirect (dative) object must take *to* if it does not come immediately after the verb.

[To + indirect object after the following adjectives.]

I am very grateful to you, etc.

I am very grateful (much obliged) to him for his help.

Marvin wants to fight a man who is superior to him.

Steve is very inferior to his father.

[To + indirect object after the following verbs.]

What had happened to him?

What did she say to her?

It appears to me that you are right.

This book belongs to my sister.

I am going to America on Saturday.

We went to England by plane.

It's time to go to bed.

He changed his mind from day to day.

He liked the idea to my surprise.

Let's drink to our future.

Can you prove to me that it is true?

She always lies to her husband.

Your boss mentioned the report to me.

He complained to the hotel about the room service.

Did your father read to you when you were young?

Translation:

He lent Mike his book.

Did you send him that letter?

_____

_____

_____

_____

_____

_____

_____

_____

_____

_____

_____

_____

_____

_____

_____

_____

_____

_____

Translation:

Certain things are common to all animals.   _____

This word is not familiar to me.   _____

This district is quite new to me.   _____

This book is very useful to me.   _____

It is evident to me that you need help.   _____

It comes natural to him.   _____

It was a hard blow to the business.   _____

David is a credit to his family.   _____

He is polite to me.   _____

Toward/towards

I walked towards her.   _____

I went to bed towards midnight.   _____

Let us hope that this is a step towards peace.   _____

Her feelings towards me are cool.   _____

Under

The cat is under the table.   _____

There's nothing new under the sun.   _____

He travelled under a false name.   _____

With

The room was filled with people.   _____

What's the matter with you?   _____

I'm not arguing with you.   _____

Go on with your story.   _____

Does Lucinda live with her uncle?   _____

I was staying wtih the Sheehans.   _____

His brother was green with envy.   _____

I bought a book with the money.   _____

He was charged with the murder.

She was in bed with a temperature.

Does this hat go with this dress?

Within

You must pay within two days.

They are within earshot, so be quiet.

Salem is within a few miles of Boston.

I live within my income.

Without

Don't go out without a hat.

It goes without saying.

I can't see without glasses.

I can't do without her.

Translation:

_____

_____

_____

_____

_____

_____

_____

_____

_____

_____

_____

Word List

able _____

absence _____

accident _____

actor _____

adjust _____

advice _____

airport _____

albums _____

alphabet _____

always _____

amount _____

anchor _____

announcer _____

annoy _____

antique _____

antiquity _____

apparently _____

appetizing _____

armchair _____

arrival _____

article _____

artist _____

ashes _____

aspirins _____

assignment _____

attack _____

attribute _____

auction _____

audience _____

auditorium _____

available _____

average _____

award _____

baffle _____

ballet _____

balloons _____

bargain _____

beach _____

beliefs _____

belt _____

biased _____

bliss _____

boots _____

boring _____

briefcase _____

brilliant _____

bucket _____

buildings _____

buses _____

bushes _____

business _____

cabinets _____

cables _____

cabs _____

cafeteria _____

calculate _____

cancel _____

cannot _____

careers _____

case _____

cast _____

celebrities _____

Centigrade _____

cereal _____

chalk _____

characteristic _____

charges _____

cheap _____

chemistry _____

chilly _____

chopsticks _____

chorus _____

circus _____

classical _____

clever _____

clients _____

closet _____

clouds _____

clubs _____

clue _____

column _____

comfortable _____

common _____

comparison _____

complex _____

composition _____

concert _____

confidence _____

confidential _____

conserve _____

constantly _____

content _____

cool _____

costs _____

costumes _____

cottage _____

counter _____

courage _____

court _____

cousin _____

crime _____

crowd _____

curiosity _____

curtain _____

customary _____

customers _____

customs agent _____

cute _____

daily _____

dance _____

dawn _____

deal _____

decrease _____

delicious _____

dentist _____

department _____

dessert _____

detective _____

diamonds _____

diet _____

difficult _____

dining room _____

diploma _____

direction _____

directions _____

distance _____

doctor _____

drawer _____

dream _____

duty _____

dynamo _____

earshot _____

echo _____

editions _____

education _____

electric mixer _____

electricity _____

electronics _____

embargo _____

enemy _____

energy _____

engine _____

engineer _____

entertain _____

envelope _____

equal _____

equipment _____

escape _____

essential _____

eternity _____

event _____

evil _____

excellent _____

exhibits _____

expensive _____

experiences _____

extremely _____

factory _____

Fahrenheit _____

fair _____

false _____

famous _____

farm _____

farm hand _____

fascinating _____

fate _____

ferry _____

fiasco _____

field _____

fierce _____

film _____

filthy _____

finally _____

finals _____

financial _____

fingerprint _____

fisherman _____

fishing rod _____

fling _____

flour _____

flute _____

foolish _____

forehead _____

forest _____

freedom _____

freeze _____

friendly _____

friendship _____

frightened _____

furniture _____

garage _____

garden _____

gate _____

gift _____

golf course _____

governor _____

grades _____

graduate _____

grateful _____

groceries _____

ground _____

guitar _____

habits _____

habitual _____

hamburgers _____

harbor _____

hardworking _____

harmonize _____

health _____

healthy _____

heaven _____

hell _____

hero _____

highways _____

hike _____

history _____

hobbies _____

hole _____

homework _____

honest _____

honors _____

horizon _____

horrible _____

hospital _____

hotel _____

hour _____

hourly _____

huge _____

human _____

humanity _____

hurdles _____

hurricane _____

husband _____

ideal _____

idiot _____

idle _____

ignorance _____

incredibly _____

industry _____

infection _____

inferior _____

influence _____

information _____

instrument _____

insurance company _____

interview _____

investigator _____

iron _____

issue _____

jacket _____

jazz _____

jet _____

journey _____

joy _____

juicy _____

just _____

kiss _____

knowledge _____

later _____

lawyer _____

leader _____

lessons _____

library _____

license _____

lies _____

lion _____

lodge _____

loose _____

lucky _____

lunch _____

magazine _____

magnificent _____

mail carrier _____

manager _____

mankind _____

manner _____

manuscripts _____

maps _____

marvelous _____

materials _____

mechanic _____

medicine _____

membership _____

million _____

mind _____

mineral water _____

mistakes _____

modern _____

monthly _____

mosquito _____

mountain climbing _____

movies _____

murder _____

museum _____

musical _____

musicians _____

mystery _____

nationality _____

native _____

nature _____

never _____

news _____

noisy _____

notebook _____

nurse _____

ocean _____

often _____

opinion _____

opposite _____

orders _____

owner _____

package _____

pancakes _____

paradise _____

particularly _____

passengers _____

passport _____

paths _____

patriotic _____

peace _____

permanent _____

person _____

photo _____

piano _____

picnic _____

pier _____

pity _____

plaid _____

plan _____

pockets _____

poisonous _____

police officer _____

popcorn _____

popular _____

pork roast _____

position _____

possible _____

postcard _____

posterity _____

potential _____

practice _____

pray _____

pride _____

prison _____

probable _____

product _____

profitable _____

providence _____

purgatory _____

purpose _____

qualities _____

racket _____

radio _____

rarely _____

recommendation _____

records _____

refrigerator _____

register _____

rehearsal _____

relatives _____

relaxation _____

religions _____

repair _____

report card _____

reporter _____

responsibility _____

restaurant _____

resumé _____

reward _____

rheumatism _____

right _____

robbery _____

roommate _____

roses _____

rules _____

rush hour _____

sailboat _____

salad _____

saucer _____

scene _____

schedules _____

sciences _____

scissors _____

scores _____

screws _____

scripts _____

search _____

seat _____

secret _____

secretary _____

seldom _____

sentry _____

sharp _____

shear _____

shoulders _____

sightsee _____

sincere _____

site _____

skis _____

skillful _____

slides _____

slim _____

slink _____

slopes _____

socialize _____

society _____

sofa _____

soldier _____

solo _____

sometimes _____

souvenir stand _____

special _____

speech _____

spoil _____

sport _____

steak _____

steeple _____

stereo _____

stomach _____

stone _____

studio _____

subject _____

succeed _____

sugar _____

suitcases _____

sunrise _____

superior _____

sure _____

surprise _____

suspicious _____

syrup _____

tacks _____

tango _____

tears _____

telegram _____

temper _____

temperature _____

tennis club _____

tension _____

textbooks _____

theater _____

thief _____

title _____

torpedo _____

tour _____

tournament _____

tow _____

town _____

traffic _____

traffic light _____

trainer _____

travel agency _____

trophy _____

troupe _____

true _____

truths _____

typewriter _____

umbrella _____

unbelievable _____

uniform _____

union _____

unsettling _____

unusual _____

upholstery _____

vacation _____

valuable _____

value _____

various _____

vases _____

wages _____

waiter _____

waltz _____

war _____

weekly _____